MAKING YOUR
FAITH
MAKE A DIFFERENCE

BARRY D. TEAGUE

While this book is intended for the reader's personal enjoyment and profit, it is also intended for group study. A leader's guide with Reproducible Sheets is available from your local bookstore or from the publisher.

VICTOR BOOKS®
A DIVISION OF SCRIPTURE PRESS PUBLICATIONS INC.
USA CANADA ENGLAND

Scripture Quotations are from *New American Standard Bible,* © The
Lockman Foundation 1960, 1962, 1963, 1968, 1971, 1972, 1973, 1975,
1977.

Library of Congress Cataloging-in-Publication Data

Teague, Barry.
    Making your faith make a difference / by Barry Teague.
        p.   cm.
    Includes bibliographical references.
    ISBN 0-89693-780-1
    1. bible, N.T. Epistles of Paul—Theology. 2. Identification (Religion)—
Biblical teaching. 3. Faith—Biblical teaching. 4. Jesus Christ—Mystical
union—Biblical teaching.
I. Title.
BS2655.I33T42   1990
234–dc20   90-31063
                                                                    CIP

1 2 3 4 5 6 7 8 9 10   Printing/Year   94 93 92 91 90

Contents

to my cherished wife Kim
and our children: Corban and Bethany

Acknowledgments

I would like to express my appreciation to Brices Creek Bible Church in general and Karen Dunlap in particular, who provided helpful interaction throughout the entirety of this project.

Foreword

Even a very casual reader of the New Testament can observe that the truth of being "in Christ" is one of the central features of the Christian life. As I observed this clear emphasis, I began to pray one of the most important prayers of my life— that the Holy Spirit would teach me all that it meant to be "in Christ." I sensed my own inability to understand this truth without divine help. Every step in grasping this spiritual reality has brought a deeper confidence in God.

I earnestly encourage you to pray this same prayer and read this book that I am confident the Holy Spirit will use to be a significant part of the answer to that prayer.

I have known Barry as a friend and have observed him in his roles as husband, father, and pastor. He has personally found this truth to be helpful in all of these responsibilities and has written *Making Your Faith Make a Difference* with a desire and prayer that you and I might also be helped in all of our relationships.

This is the kind of book that needs to be written and then read by God's people. Barry presents doctrine as living truth. He not only states his points clearly, but he also illustrates and applies them in a way that makes reading this book enjoyable and edifying. God can use it to open up to you an understanding of the spiritual truth of the entire New Testament. The book will also be a helpful resource to refer to as you study your Bible.

It is my prayer that the Lord will send a season of spiritual refreshment to the church in this century. The illumination of the truth of being "in Christ" will no doubt be an invaluable contribution to this spiritual work that only God can do. May you find genuine fellowship with our Lord Jesus in your reading of this book.

Dr. Bill Thrasher
Moody Bible Institute

Introduction

Dr. Charles Ryrie spoke of our identification in Christ as probably the most important truth undergirding our spiritual life. Unfortunately, "this concept," he wrote, "is little understood, unbalanced in its presentation and unused in application."[1]

There was a time in my life when I would sit in class and wonder whether there was anything that made me different from those in the class who did not know Christ as their Saviour. And if so, would they recognize it? What I was really struggling with in my own elementary way was "Is my Christianity making a difference in my life?" More often than not, I had to conclude it wasn't.

Now, as many Christians come through my doors for counseling, I find that they too are asking the same question: "Why is it that when my Christianity should be making the greatest difference in my outlook, attitude, or actions, it leaves only faint impressions?"

Surely, God has designed our faith for more, but where do we go for answers? The tendency is to jump on some faddish bandwagon of spirituality. Though we may be able to ride the wave for a while, it usually comes crashing down on us, and we are left strung out and disillusioned.

It was this quest for real answers which over the years drove me to the very heart of God's re-creative work. Paul described it succinctly as being "in Christ."

Prior to Paul's conversion, the sphere of his life had been

centered "in Judaism" (Gal. 1:13-14). Within this sphere he sought security and significance. Though he boasted in his glorious heritage, honed his intellectual genius, and fed his religious zeal, none of it brought fulfillment.

Then one day on a journey to Damascus, all that changed, along with Paul's explanation of how to live. A compendium of this dramatic change is found in Galatians 2:20. Paul says, "I have been crucified with Christ; and it is no longer I who live, but Christ lives in me; and the life which I now live in the flesh I live by faith in the Son of God, who loved me, and delivered Himself up for me."

What a powerful word—*crucified*. Something happened on that Damascus road which caused Paul to see that everything which had defined living for him—everything he had stood for, everything he had believed in, everything he felt had made him who he was or ever would be—it all met a ruthless death. It could never again hold for him the key to living. In its place emerged a new life and a new sphere described in two short words: IN CHRIST.

Paul's tremendous understanding of who he was in Christ became his anchor. As a result, he spent his life growing in, not groping for, spiritual maturity. This understanding of who we are in Christ is where we too must begin.

Prior to accepting Christ as Saviour, your sphere of security and identity may have been in business and finances, in romance and sexual conquest, in education and prestige, or in some other pursuit of fulfillment. But at the moment of salvation, God, by a decisive act of His grace, placed you in Christ.

This identification marks a radical change and departure from all that you were before. In Colossssians 1:13-14 we read that we have been transferred from the kingdom of darkness into the kingdom of the beloved Son. James Stewart wrote that a person in Christ "has been lifted out of the cramping restrictions of his earthly lot into a totally different sphere, the sphere of Christ. He has been transplanted into a new soil and a new climate, and both soil and climate are Christ."[2]

This new environment and radical change haunted me over the years and caused me to begin my own odyssey into this glorious theme. As I studied each epistle of Paul, I was amazed to discover that my new life in Christ (1) determines my possessions, (2) dictates my practice, and (3) details my prospect for the future. Furthermore, I came to see that these three facets of identification in Christ were the major building blocks on which maturity is built.

My twofold prayer for you is that you will first come to understand and appreciate more fully who you are in Christ, and second, that you will be challenged to meditate on and personally apply these truths to your life.

In Christ,

Barry D. Teague

Possessing a New Heritage

In day-to-day living, there is a subtle seduction to build our identity or self-esteem on performance or ability. Everywhere we go, the world reinforces this message.

But the Bible says the proper basis for self-worth is resting upon who we are in Christ. Everything we read in the Bible reinforces this message. Our identity in Christ is not merely a "future phenomenon." Rather, it is a present reality of rich spiritual heritage which the Lord has already pressed into our hands. Part One will teach us the difference these possessions can and do make in our lives.

First, by virtue of my identification in Christ, I have been totally forgiven and cleansed by God. I do not have to be haunted by past failures. Second, I have a freedom in Christ which brings about a different orientation to sin. Though I am not exempt from sin's influence at this time, I have been released from its tyranny. Third, I have a holiness in Christ which translates into an assurance of the ongoing presence and work of the Holy Spirit in my life. Fourth, I have been given every spiritual blessing in Christ. These blessings are mine regardless of my talents or capabilities. Furthermore, I possess these blessings to the same degree as all my other brothers and sisters in Christ do. I may or may not be viewed as a second-class citizen on earth, but in Christ, God has given me first-class status forever. Lastly, I have been given a life of fulfillment in Christ. I do not have to go outside Christ for self-esteem. In Him I am complete. Rather than inhibiting productivity and accomplishment, my completeness in Christ provides the right matrix out of which they may properly flow.

one

Romans:
When God Pardons in Christ

Years ago a traveling salesman whose territory covered the British Isles discovered that on one extended trip he would be in three Scottish cities on successive weekends. He was thrilled at the opportunity because in each of the three cities resided one of the outstanding preachers of his day. He knew that with a little effort and good timing, he could hear each of them preach. In his journal he related the impressions each left upon him.

In St. Andrews I heard a tall, stately man preach, and he showed me the majesty of God. I afterwards heard a little fair man preach, and he showed me the loveliness of Christ. I then went to Irvine, where I heard preach a well-favoured, proper old man, with a long beard, and that man showed me all my heart.[1]

In one sense this is a microcosm of the entire Word of God in general and the Book of Romans in particular: the heart of sinful man, the sovereign initiative of God, and the loveliness of the work of Christ. The emphasis throughout the New Testament rests not so much on what sinful men did to Jesus, but on what Jesus did for sinful man—the loveliness of His work. Never is this truer than in Romans.

When we focus on the Book of Romans and begin to consider what Jesus did for sinful man, we must start with one word: *justification*. The word concerns itself with how a person can stand righteous (be just) before a holy God. It ties together the three truths mentioned earlier: (1) man's depravity, (2) God's initiative, and (3) Christ's compassionate work.

MAN'S DEPRAVITY

There is a German term which is entering the American vocabulary: *angst*. Though the term is new to us, what it describes is not. It speaks of that indefinable inner anxiety, that drumbeat of dissonance within every heart. Strip away the bravura of locker-room conversations and you will hear the empty echo of *angst*. Unplug the living-room TV and you will see the darkness of *angst*. *Angst* is all around us because alienation is all around us. No matter how hard we try, we cannot shake free of it.

A NAGGING REALITY
Down through the ages man has had to face the nagging realization that there is some sort of alienation between him and God. Job faced it. And the rich young ruler in Matthew 19 sought out Jesus because of it. It has been felt equally by those secluded in the highest mansions of Beverly Hills and those who sleep in the streets.

In the face of such alienation, the smoldering question remains, "How can I, a sinner, be at peace with God?" The opening chapters of Romans show that man's own ability and ingenuity cannot possibly lead to justification before God. It is a task no man can master, a hurdle no man can jump. Chapters 1–3 chronicle the failure of man before God. Whether Jew or Gentile, free or slave, fool or wise, none measure up. None can claim the stamp of "justified," whether he approaches his religion with inward diligence or outward disdain. As much as we would like to maneuver around it, the solemn indictment of Romans still stands: "For all have sinned and fall short of the glory of God" (3:23).

SIN EXPOSED

In light of such a pronouncement, we would surely be helped if we could clarify the meaning of sin. The Hebrews used a word for sin, *hata*, that was connected with the skill of hunting. If a man shot an arrow and missed the mark (the bull's-eye), his friend might lean over his shoulder and say, "hata!" In other words, "Sorry, you missed the mark. You sinned."

To sin is not necessarily to do some grossly diabolical deed but rather to simply miss the mark of life that God has established—glorifying Him. In all my contacts with people, I have yet to meet someone who says he has always lived up to his own goals or standards. Well, if we cannot hit the bull's-eye of our own standards, we need no persuasive argument to convince us that we could never hit God's. None of us has measured up. This is the irrefutable evidence for what the Bible calls sin.

Sin is in us all. I read of a little boy who stole five dollars from his father, and when he owned up to his sin, his father was furious. But after the father calmed down, he lifted his son up on his lap and began to share a little confession of his own. He told his son that when he was a little boy, he had stolen a dozen eggs from his mother and sold them. The little boy put his arms around his father's neck and said, "Dad, we are partners together, aren't we?" His surprised father stammered back, "Whaaat do you mean?" The little boy responded, "Why, we are both thieves."

Candid and to the point, this illustration speaks directly to the plight of mankind. The noted historian Arnold Toynbee acknowledged, "There must be a vein of original sin in human nature. Civilization is only a thin cake of custom overlying a molten mess of wickedness always boiling up for an opportunity to burst out."[2] You see, the real question isn't: "How much have I fallen short?" or "When have I fallen short?" The real question is: "When haven't I fallen short of God's glory?"

Measure the best of us at our very best, and you will still find that none come close to God's standard. This is what it means to be depraved. And this is the state of man's heart. Only when we feel the tug of such a heart condition will we understand J.I. Packer's warning: "True religion does not begin till the question presses: how may I get rid of my sins?"[3]

GOD'S SOVEREIGN INITIATIVE

If there were ever a problem which only God could solve, the justification of sinful man is it. Therefore it is time for our best efforts and promises to exit, and God to take center stage.

Romans 3:24 shows the initiative of God commanding the spotlight. God acted to justify us, "as a gift by His grace." The Greek word *dōreā* rendered by the phrase "as a gift" in Romans 3:24 is also translated in John 15:25 as "without a cause." So, the fullest meaning of Romans 3:24 would be: "Being justified as a gift, without a cause found in man, but solely by His grace."

This verse leaves no maneuvering for sinful man. Nothing within our hearts could have obligated God to rescue us. Clearly, the cause for action rested entirely on the loving shoulders of God. Deeply imbedded within His own heart was His desire to act graciously, to act lovingly, to act freely, and to act on behalf of helpless man. This is what the initiative of God is all about. Had He not acted, justification would have been nothing more than "a tale told by an idiot, full of sound and fury, signifying nothing."

CHRIST'S COMPASSIONATE WORK

The question might be asked, "But if God chose to be gracious, why didn't He simply ignore man's sinfulness? After all, who could overrule the Moral Judge of the Universe?" Yet it is precisely because of who He is that He could not overlook sin. Imagine the public outcry over a judge who whimsically decided that rape, thievery, or murder would no longer be punishable offenses and that moral evil no longer mattered. We would demand that this judge be dismissed as unworthy and unrighteous.

Had God treated sin casually, He would have become the chief perverter of righteousness rather than its protector and provider, for if He could ignore sin, He could ignore righteousness as well. This would render for naught the all important work of Christ on our behalf and put our eternal destiny in the greatest of peril.

CHRIST·ACCOMPLISHES REDEMPTION

If sin could not be ignored, how then could a loving and just God accomplish His plan of justifying us? This is the precise question raised in Romans 3:26. The answer is found succinctly tucked away in seed form in the last phrase of Romans 3:24. God has justly justified the sinner "through the redemption which is in Christ Jesus."

Before us stands that choice phrase of Paul—"in Christ." The term is used twenty-one times throughout Romans, but its first appearance is in 3:24. Such a judicious beginning serves to heighten its central role in the process of justification. It is as if Paul has been saving up for three chapters, as he chronicles man's failures, waiting for that one special moment to announce to needy souls everywhere: "There is a solution to your problem and it is found *in Christ.*"

Everything depends on Christ. Through His death on the cross, He has redeemed us from our sinful condition. The punishment that Isaiah says should have rightly fallen on us, He has mercifully borne on the cross (Isa. 53:6). At the moment we receive Christ, God provides us with the raiment of Christ's own righteousness, and we stand justified and at peace with God (Rom. 5:1).

CHRIST'S UNIQUE WORK
He was fully God.
The work of justification demanded one who was both fully God and fully man. It was God's glory that had been marred

so it was God's glory that had to be restored. To stand righteous before God requires more than a good effort, it requires God's glory. Who but God could meet such a standard? If Jesus Christ is any less than God, we would be journeying on a bridge which still remains incomplete for the final span.

He was fully man.
But Jesus Christ had to be wholly man as well. It was man who had rebelled against God, and it was man's sins that had to be judged; therefore it was man who had to pay the price. If Christ were to mediate for sinful man, He had to be a man. This is why the New Testament, when explaining His work as mediator, always stresses His manhood: "For there is one God, and one mediator also between God and men, the man Christ Jesus" (1 Tim. 2:5).

He alone transforms the irreparable.
I came out of my study one afternoon to find my son, then only two years old, working feverishly. The plastic steering wheel on his toy had broken off at the top of the plastic shaft. Time and time again he would place the broken steering wheel in its proper place with the same futile results. It simply would not stay attached. Finally, he looked up and helplessly handed me the steering wheel saying, "Here, Daddy, fix it please." I stooped down and pretended to try, but I knew it was broken beyond repair.

There was, however, something my wife and I could do. We took him to a store and bought him a new riding toy. His delight was evident in the thrill in his voice. He had left the house with nothing but an irreparable toy, but he returned with one that was new and better.

This is what the saving grace of God in Christ has done for us. We take the brokenness of our sinful lives and childishly keep trying to make it all fit back together. We may glue it and dress it up, but inwardly we know it is all a facade. The brokenness of sin and alienation from God remains.

All the while a loving God looks on. He has not ignored

our plight. He has sought a way to restore us (Rom. 4:5). He has sent His Son. Christ's death was the great cost of love's intervention. Now God is waiting—waiting to replace the irreplaceable, waiting to re-create us as new creatures in Christ.

God's initiative and Christ's compassionate work came together to secure for us a righteous standing before God. The Bible tells us that we may enter into this standing "through faith in Jesus Christ" (Rom. 3:22). Faith is the passageway through which the work of Christ is applied to our hearts. God is ready to intervene with the work of His Son, but He will not force His intervention on us. Just as my son had to look up to me, we must first individually look up to Him with the acknowledgment of our own helplessness. It is only as we turn to Him in faith that God righteously places us in the heart of His Son and pronounces: "Justified in Christ!" Romans 3:24 tells us that this transaction takes place not at some distant and uncertain future, but at the first fledgling moment of our new life in Christ. As the Greek scholar F.F. Bruce remarked: "God pronounces a man righteous at the beginning of his course, not at the end of it."[4]

Yes, Romans 3:23 gives the solemn pronouncement on all mankind, but Romans 3:24 bears the greater and irrevocable pronouncement of God on those who believe: *Justified in Christ*.

IMPLICATIONS OF BEING JUSTIFIED IN CHRIST

"I'm justified in Christ!" It sounds too good to be true. It runs contrary to all the years of guilt and frustration. Accepting this statement as true, however, will not automatically create a difference in the way we live and view ourselves. We must understand what God means by such a pronouncement.

Dr. Roy Gustefson provides an excellent illustration that helps us unfold some of the dazzling splendor of being justified in Christ. A man in England once decided to catch the ferry to the Continent for a vacation. Being rich, he naturally brought along his Rolls-Royce. While he was on the Continent, his Rolls-Royce had a mechanical breakdown. Not knowing exactly what to do, he cabled the company back in England for some guidance. Well, they went right to work. They flew a mechanic over with all the necessary equipment. He fixed the car and then flew back to England, leaving the Rolls-Royce owner free to continue his vacation.

The man was thankful for the prompt service but wondered what kind of bill he was going to receive. When he returned to England and discovered he had not been sent a bill, he wrote a letter asking how much he owed. Finally, someone in the company responded with a note which read: *Dear Sir: There is no record anywhere in our files that anything ever went wrong with a Rolls-Royce.*[5]

NO DEBT

Now that is justification with a capital *J*. The story illustrates two very important truths of what God has done for us in Christ. The first is that God has already paid the debt. We no longer owe a red cent on our scarlet sins. If you were to write a letter to God asking Him how much you owe for all your sins now that you have put your faith in Christ, He would send back the note of Romans 8:1: "There is therefore now no condemnation for those who are in Christ Jesus." In simple English that means *no debt*. God aggressively declares that all who are in Christ are not guilty. The debt has been paid and canceled in the blood of His Son.

Why are we so slow to accept this? The answer must lie in the fact that we have an accuser (Rev. 12:10) who will do anything and everything to keep us from feeling this sense of reconciliation and peace with God.. He majors in pointing out our flaws and making us feel guilty and condemned. Thankfully, he does not have the last word.

Romans 8 could well be titled, "The Overruling Gavel of God." When Satan comes and says, "How can you call yourself a Christian after what you have done?" God responds, "I'm for him, and if I am for him, who can be against him?" (See v. 31.)

Now if we have sinned, we need to confess our sins honestly and wholeheartedly, but we can do so without the foreboding sense of condemnation that Satan would like to heap on us. The reference point of confession becomes crucial. Our confession now originates from a point of companionship, not alienation. What a comfort to know that God is for us.

Furthermore, we have the assurance of Christ's intercession in heaven on our behalf (Rom. 8:34). This assurance of intercession reminds us that at that crisis moment when heaven and hell seem to hang in the balance and Satan threatens to expose the horrible sins of our past, Christ comes to our rescue. He leans over to the Father and says in essence, "Father, I paid it all; he owes no debt!"

What can the world, the flesh, and the devil possibly uncover about you that has not been covered by the blood of Christ? Nothing. What could they find that would be grounds for separating you from the love of God? Nothing. Paul exhausted all the options when he wrote in Romans 8:38-39: "For I am convinced that neither death, nor life, nor angels, nor principalities, nor things present, nor things to come, nor powers, nor height, nor depth, nor any other created thing, shall be able to separate us from the love of God, which is in Christ Jesus our Lord."

God's gavel bangs and the objections are overruled. He has placed us in Christ and nothing can dislodge us from His eternal mooring of love.

It is critical for our Christian growth that we understand this truth, believe it, and apply it. Too often we live as though our relationship with God dangles by the thinnest of threads. We act as if we have observed God tearing up our debt to Him only to see Him turn around and inform us that He had actually done nothing more than tear up a copy. The original remains locked away in some heavenly vault, awaiting His closer scrutiny.

No wonder so many of us experience so little joy. We act as if we have received little more than a stay of execution rather than full acquittal. Such news might bring temporary relief but proves incapable of promoting any lasting joy. Justification in Christ, however, means nothing less than full acquittal.

I will never forget when God comforted me with this great truth. It was the turning point of my spiritual walk. Though I had accepted Christ during my early teens, I had gone for years with no assurance of my relationship with God. I had the warped perspective that my hard work for God would keep Him near. Yet, deep within my heart lingered the nagging realization that I could never measure up, never work hard enough. Then the fear would set in. I figured that one day God would look through my veneer and, not liking what He'd see, check out of my life like my father had done years earlier. It was a frustrating paradox that left me emotionally and physically spent. If, as I felt, my earthly father did not see anything in me worth sticking around for, how could I pretend that my Heavenly Father would do otherwise?

How wrong I was! In college someone shared with me the infinitely more stable promises of God. I began to draw comfort and strength from statements such as: "I will never desert you, nor will I ever forsake you" (Heb. 13:5). But the verse which brought peace to my heart and renewed joy to my life was Romans 8:1: "There is therefore now no condemnation for those who are in Christ Jesus." I realized as never before that the debt had already been paid. God did not find it hard to forgive me. The hard part was accomplished on a hill outside Jerusalem. I now stood in Christ accepted and pardoned—His child forever.

How thrilling to realize the power of the Cross to remove forever the burden of sin and guilt. A Southern Baptist evangelist from my home state of North Carolina spoke about coming back to his hometown after being gone for a few years. He was in a department store trying on clothes when a former high school teacher recognized him. Here's what transpired:

> She said to me, "Are you Gene Ridley?"
> I said, "Yes, Ma'am."
> She said, "They tell me you're making a preacher."
> I said, "I am."

"Are you still preaching?"
They always say still. *They expect me to cash it in any-time. I said, "Yea, I'm still preaching."*
"Well, I'd never thought you'd have been a preacher. I remember what you used to be."
And I thought, Old gal, you'd better be proud of yourself. You can do something God can't do."[6]

What a timeless truth: no debt. The haunting failures of our lives are gone. Sin which lay as an intolerable burden on us has been removed not only from our conscience, but also from the very presence of God.

NO RECORD
One more important truth concerning our justification in Christ comes from the illustration of the Rolls-Royce. The owner was anticipating a huge bill; however, the note he received indicated he owed nothing and affirmed there was no record of brokenness in the files.

What a thrill to discover that God has done more than promise to remember our sins no more. In Christ, He views us as if we had never sinned at all! Everything has been made completely right, and no record of brokenness remains.

Is this mere "legal fiction" or a case of doctoring up the records a la Watergate? The answer is no for one very simple reason—the records of justification are safely tucked away in Christ. When God looks into His Son, He can see but one thing: righteousness, the bull's-eye of His own glory. Since He looks at us through Christ, He invariably sees the same. This is the truth behind the "great exchange" of 2 Corinthians 5:21: "He made Him who knew no sin to be sin on our behalf, that we might become the righteousness of God in Him." The Father compassionately wrapped our sins around Christ on the cross so that He might cover us with the Son's robe of righteousness.

One day in London thousands of people assembled to watch British soldiers march by in a parade. A father decided to take his son to the building where he worked, and there, high above the crowds, selected a window which lent the best possible view. Soon the soldiers appeared, proudly displaying their brilliant uniforms. The little boy, awed by such an impressive sight, tugged on his father's pants legs and exclaimed, "Those are the purest and most beautiful white uniforms I have ever seen!"

Without looking down the father said, "You mean red, brilliant red uniforms, don't you?"

"Oh no," said the little boy. "They are white, just as white as snow."

Well, that simply could not be. When the father bent down to explain the difference between red and white, he happened to notice a band of red glass around the lower section of the window through which his son had been peering. Anyone who looks at a red object through red glass, can't help but see the object as pure white, so from the boy's vantage point, the soldiers' uniforms were indeed as white as snow.

Around 700 B.C. Isaiah had prophesied, "Though your sins are as scarlet, they will be as white as snow; though they are red like crimson, they will be like wool" (1:18). Perhaps for all the long intervening years the people wondered how a just God was going to accomplish such an amazing feat. Perhaps you have wondered the same. While man sat and pondered, God initiated a marvelous plan. By applying the blood of Christ to our sins He would assure His righteousness on us forever (Rom. 3:22). In short, He would justify us in Christ. This is why Christ could promise that He would present us without "spot or wrinkle or any such thing" (Eph. 5:27). We are spotless because we are in the spotless One. What a plan! What a promise!

You never again have to shrink from fear of condemnation. Let the world accuse. Let objections fly. Let them invite God to look again and again to see if He can detect the red stain of guilt and sin in your life. There is nothing to fear. Because you are perfect and without sin? No! But because you know God will silence all the accusations and shouts of condemnation by peering through the blood of His Son and concluding: "Just as I thought, white. White as snow."

OUR RESPONSE TO JUSTIFICATION

Justification involves the inability of man, the divine initiative of God, and the compassionate work of Christ. It means that when we accepted Christ's work by faith, we were immediately placed into Christ, in whose righteousness we shall forever stand without condemnation or record of sin.

But does this truth give us license to sin? Paul answered that in Romans 6:1-2 when he declared, "Are we to continue in sin that grace might increase? May it never be! How shall we who died to sin still live in it?" Mark it well, if justification leads to loose living, you either do not have it or you do not understand it.

When we follow Paul through the argument of Romans, we find that the pronouncement of justification in Christ actually leads away from sin into a deepening commitment to God. Romans 12:1 urges the believer "by the mercies of God [seen first and foremost in the justification of sinful men in Christ] to present your bodies a living and holy sacrifice, acceptable to God, which is your spiritual service of worship." On the heels of justification comes a life of thankful presentation.

As a college freshman, my awareness of a righteousness in Christ was like the dawning of spring after the long, wintery years of *angst*. The chore of living for Christ was replaced with the joy of Christ living in me. To present my life to Him seemed the most reasonable, proper, and exciting thing I could ever do. After all the intervening years, it still does. It will forever remain the only honest choice for anyone who has been justified in Christ!

As wonderful as justification in Christ is, it does not begin to tell the whole story of what we have been given in Christ. There is yet much more that the work of Christ has accomplished for us.

two

Galatians:
Freedom in Christ

Recently I was speaking to a group of college students. I asked, "How many of you would like to be free from a bad habit?" They all raised their hands. Somehow I suspect that every person reading this book would as well. So where do we turn for help?

A few years ago *Penthouse* magazine took out large advertisements in newspapers around the country to accuse those seeking to enact antipornography laws of trying to restrict Americans' freedom. These advertisements encouraged people to patronize stores that still displayed *Penthouse* openly on the racks.

The advertisers sought to sell us on the idea that freedom rests in the ability to do anything you wish. But is this really freedom? Behind the slick marketing techniques lie two fundamental questions: What is freedom? Where is freedom to be found?

WHAT IS FREEDOM?

FREEDOM: NOT A GAME WITHOUT RULES
If we try to find the city of Freedom while skipping down the road of no restraints, we will never get there. We will

find instead a greater enslavement: bondage to the path of passions and the power of least resistance.

Suppose a man decided to exercise the freedom of no restraints by climbing up to the top of the Empire State Building and jumping off. For the first several stories he would have an initial feeling of euphoria. He has no restraints, no restrictions, no hang-ups. He certainly appears free and unencumbered. But suppose, ten stories from the ground, you stick your head out a window and shout to the man: "It's great that you're so free, but now are you free to stop the fall and avoid the consequences?" He now has but ten stories left to review his definition of freedom.

Even many who would not align themselves with Christian ideals have come to recognize that such an understanding of freedom leads only to greater bondage. George Leonard was known as one of the founders of the sexual revolution of the late '60s, yet in a book written in the early '80s entitled *The End of Sex* he writes: "What I have learned is that there are no games without rules."[1] This is a powerful commentary on what freedom is not: a game without rules!

FREEDOM: BECOMING WHAT YOU SHOULD BE
If freedom is not the ability to do whatever you wish, what is it? In the early part of this century Paul de Lagarde asserted: "He is not free who can do what he wills, but rather he who can become what he should be."[2] At the heart of freedom resides this ability to become what we were created to be.

Immediately a question comes to mind: Do we know what we should become? In almost prophetic words Helmut Thielicke reminds us: "Our understanding of freedom is threatened with disintegration because we do not know what 'we should become.' "[3]

To discover what we should become, we must turn to the Bible. It is a record of God creatively designing man in His own image to live a fulfilling life of fellowship with Him and to be His children forever. This is the creative purpose for man.

Obviously something has gone wrong. As I was on my

way to a nearby college to speak, I stopped to buy some breath mints. In front of me was a young man gearing up for the evening carrying several six-packs of beer. While I stood in line, I thought, *G.K. Chesterton was right: "Whatever else is or is not true, this one thing is certain—man is not what he was meant to be."*[4]

A prime example of man having lost his way and his freedom can be witnessed at the turn of every New Year. How many of us have kept our New Year's resolutions? And if you did, did you really change or just replace one bad habit with another? How many people have quit drinking only to pick up smoking? How many have quit smoking only to pick up twenty or thirty pounds of extra weight in a year? To be sure, some habits are more detrimental than others, but any bad habit thrusts us into a vicious cycle of enslavement to sin. In our natural state we are slaves in the worst of ways. We find ourselves desperately muttering the words of Paul, "Who will set me free?" (Rom. 7:24)

WHERE IS FREEDOM FOUND?

Time and again Paul experienced the frustration of "not practicing what I would like to do, but . . . doing the very thing I hate" (Rom. 7:15).

Many of us can identify with his frustration. The problem lies in the destructive web of sin. What we need is something or someone who can produce in us a freedom of liberation, restoration, and enablement—a freedom that will restore God's creative design.

FREEDOM BY THE LAW? NO
Some try to attain God's design by slavish devotion to good works. Paul certainly tried this. And though by human standards he was found blameless, he realized that such devotion would never bring about freedom (Phil. 3:1-8). In Galatians 2:19 he states: "For through the Law I died to the Law, that I might live to God." A few years ago I read of a young man who, because of a misguided understanding of Jesus' teach-

ing, cut off his right hand and gouged out his right eye in a desperate attempt to free himself from sin's bondage. But his sincere though terribly misguided efforts proved powerless. He was incapable of setting himself free by such slavish devotion to the Law. And so are we.

The reason for our inadequacy lies in the fact that the Law was never intended to initiate freedom. Paul acknowledged this truth in Galatians 3:21-26. The Law did little more than reveal sin. At best, it could only enflame hearts with a desire to escape sin's oppressive grip. But as far as initiating freedom, it simply could not produce. Such an act was beyond its capabilities.

John Bunyan's *Pilgrim's Progress* beautifully illustrates this truth. The main character, Christian, finds himself in the Interpreter's house. There is a large room covered with dust. A young man, broom in hand, enters the room and starts to sweep. Rather than cleaning the room, he sends the dust flying, and those in the room gag for fresh air. Then the Interpreter calls for a young girl nearby to bring some water and sprinkle it across the room. Her actions succeed in settling the dust and bring immediate relief to everyone.

The Interpreter explained. The dust was the ever-present sinfulness of man's heart. The young man was the Law. The Law could not prevent the lusts of the flesh, it could only reveal their presence. The room desperately needed someone to come in and sprinkle some water over the dust to settle it. Only then would the broom be of any profit. The water was the liberating message of grace in Jesus Christ.[5]

FREEDOM IN CHRIST? YES
The Interpreter had grasped the teaching of the New Testament concerning freedom. The verb employed in the New Testament for "freedom" is *eleutheroō*. This verb bears a potent message which is very clear, precise, and yes, quite exclusive. *Eleutheroō* is used solely for the act which occurs or has occurred through Jesus Christ; therefore, according to the New Testament, the birthplace of real freedom rests solely in Christ. You will not find it anywhere else.

Until we come to Christ we are bound by the shackles of guilt, sin, and frustration. We are slaves to passion and the law of least resistance. We are not free from sin. We are not free to become what we were created to be. We are not free to live to God.

Only in Christ can the heart's cry for freedom be satisfied. This path of freedom in Christ is the focus of the Book of Galatians. Eight times Paul uses the phrase "in Christ." The majority of these references underscore one central truth: when sinners accept Christ, they have found entrance into the realm of genuine freedom. Galatians 5:1 puts it best, "It was for freedom that Christ set us free."

Christ achieved what all the resolutions, gimmicks, and good works had failed to do. He met the requirements necessary to produce true freedom.

Christ: the liberator.

Galatians 4:3-5 indicates that we were held in bondage to the world's way of thinking and doing things, but the coming of Christ won deliverance for us.

The verb *to redeem,* found in verse 5, is a term we need to understand. When you go shopping, you can buy merchandise on lay-away. Though it bears your name, it remains in the store until you have made the final payment. This is one form of redemption.

However, the word used here, *exagorazō,* sketches a more thorough picture. It suggests someone entering the store, purchasing the item, and immediately removing it from the marketplace so that the store has no more control over it. The transaction is seen as totally complete and absolutely final.

This is what Christ has done for us. At conversion He bought us from the black market of hell and immediately removed us to the new environment of heaven. Galatians 1:4 tells us that Christ "gave Himself for our sins, that He might deliver us out of this present evil age." This act of deliverance is a present reality. He did not redeem us only to leave us unprotected and vulnerable. Rather, He broke the power of sin over us by taking us right out of the marketplace of hell and placing us securely in the confines of His own heart. We no longer need to be bound by past tragedies, present circumstances, or future fears. Christ has severed the chains, and any influence they may seek to exert on us no longer originates from a position of dominating authority over us but rather from our willingness to rest in Christ's enabling grace (which we will treat more fully in the next few pages).

Suffice it to say that at this point bondage to sin was the first hurdle that had to be overcome if we were to find freedom. Christ accomplished this. But He has done so much more.

Christ: the restorer.

Freedom, as we have already seen, is more than just freedom *from*, it is also freedom to *become*. Galatians 4:5-7 shows Christ inaugurating the positive side of freedom "that He might redeem those who were under the Law, that we might receive the adoption as sons. And because you are sons, God has sent forth the Spirit of His Son into our hearts, crying, 'Abba! Father!' Therefore you are no longer a slave, but a son; and if a son, then an heir through God."

We were created for an eternal and fulfilling relationship with God. That destiny was forfeited because of rebellion and subsequent enslavement to sin. But Jesus has brought true freedom back into focus. He has redeemed us from corruption and reestablished us in righteousness. Before, we lived in servitude to sin, but now in Christ, we live as children and heirs. In Christ we are liberated; in Christ we are restored. Galatians 5:1 proclaims: "It was for freedom that Christ set us free; therefore keep standing firm and do not be subject again to a yoke of slavery."

Galatians 5:1 is both comforting and confrontational. It issues a call to stand firm against the yoke of slavery. Here a crucial point emerges. We are free in Christ and are assured of being so for all eternity. We have been liberated and restored to a loving, nurturing relationship with our Heavenly Father. Yet the daily experience of that freedom is contingent on our standing firm.

In other words, freedom goes hand in hand with obedience. Obedience does not initially sound much like freedom, does it? Not if we swallow the false definition of freedom as "doing whatever we want to." But when freedom is properly understood, boundaries are not only right but necessary. Helmut Thielicke remarked that "real freedom is a bondage and nothing else. The chains of unfreedom are broken . . . by entering into a genuine commitment to, and acceptance of, obligations that sustain one's very existence. Therefore the difference between unfreedom and freedom is not the difference between being bound and unbound, but rather between false and true bondage."[6]

As contrary as it may sound, it takes obedience to enjoy true freedom. Quite frankly, this is illustrated all around us. I can sit down at a piano day after day, and proclaim, "I'm free!" and proceed to bang any old key. But is the result genuine freedom or absolute chaos? Freedom to become a great pianist and freedom to play and enjoy beautiful music can only be achieved by years of practice, discipline, and obedience to the basic principles of music.

Since it is at this point of obedience that failure rather than freedom so often appears to be the norm, the tendency is to think that Christ's work of liberation and restoration was nothing more than a cosmetic freedom—the kind of freedom which is long on theory and short on practical implementation. But before we throw up our hands in despair, we need to realize that Christ has become not only our restorer and liberator but also our enabler.

Christ: the enabler.

The difference between obedience when we were outside Christ and obedience now that we are in Christ is God's provision of special spiritual enablement. He has not abandoned us to our own strength. In addition to having been set free from enslavement to sin and restored to a positive loving relationship with God, we have also been assured of the constant enablement of the Holy Spirit for the temptations and trials ahead. Galatians 5:13-26 shows that Christ has mapped out a course of action for us to undertake and given us the Holy Spirit as our faithful and overcoming guide along the way.

Galatians 5:13 reads, "You were called [destined] to freedom, brethren; only do not turn your freedom into an opportunity for the flesh, but through love serve one another." All of us have known the bullying techniques of the flesh from time to time. Often it seems that the more we determine not to be intimidated, the quicker we succumb to disobedience.

For instance, when you were outside Christ and someone hurt you, you probably looked for an opportunity to strike back. Your attack may have been clandestine, like gloating with satisfaction when the one who hurt you fell on his face. You might have made a frontal attack, seeking to humiliate him before others. Worse yet, your anger may have escalated to a physically violent confrontation. Regardless of the form, the one constant was a real and consuming desire for retaliation.

But now, in Christ, you are finally free to choose a course of action that was impossible before. You are free to respond in Christlike love! You have received assurance of the Holy Spirit's guidance and power at work in you to develop the ability and discipline to choose Christlike love. Galatians 5:16 reminds us to "walk by the Spirit, and you will not carry out the desire of the flesh."

In 1986 I asked the Bitterman family to come share with our church about the life of their son, Chet, who was a Wycliffe missionary to Columbia. As they spoke, I came to a greater understanding of the enabling work of Christ.

In 1981, at the young age of 27, Chet was killed by the M-19 guerrilla movement that was trying to force Wycliffe out of the country. Only hours after Chet's murder, a Colombian radio station made a live telephone hookup with Chet's parents in Pennsylvania. In this emotional interview, his parents were asked how they felt about the tragedy. Their response flowed through the streets of Bogota and cut through the dense jungles of that beautiful country.

His father spoke first. "I don't know what God plans to do with the death of my son. I guess we'll just have to wait and find out. I'm sorry I won't see Chet again in this life, but I know I'll see him again in heaven. Chet had a great love for the Columbian people; he wanted to tell the Indians about God. Now, I'm hoping someone else will go in his place."

His mother spoke next with deep conviction. "What do we say to the Columbian people? Just that we love them. This gives us no ill feelings toward Colombia or Colombians. God loves them. So do we. We're hoping the guerrillas come to know God."[7]

I thought as I heard these remarks that this is where the real sounds of freedom peal. In Christ we have found our liberation, our restoration, and our enablement. We are not bound to the past but are free to choose the path of love under the guidance of the Holy Spirit. This is being all you can be!

IMPLICATIONS OF FREEDOM IN CHRIST

AFFECTING PUBLIC EVILS

The implications of this freedom touch us at every level of life. Our freedom has a direct bearing on how we approach social reform.

We are hearing a lot about liberation theology these days. Some are parading Marxism with the veneer of Christianity—all in the name of freedom. But once again let us remember the words of Helmut Thielicke: "Our understanding of freedom is threatened with disintegration because we do not know what 'we should become.'" Can Marxism ever set someone free to become a child of God? Marxism sees man as nothing more than dialectic materialism, whereas Christianity sees man as an immortal soul worthy of personal dignity, respect, and redemption. How much is dialectic materialism worth? How much can it 'become'? In Jesus Christ, however, we come to see the real value of man's worth; we come to see what man may become.

Therefore we can and should stand against the evils of

abortion, pornography, child abuse, and social injustices. But our stance must find its footing firmly planted upon the rock of the liberating person of Jesus Christ and not in some slippery and false view of man.

Furthermore, when the social involvement shifts from a political or cultural agenda to a spiritual one, it thereby alters with great decisiveness the methods we should employ to promote change (Zech. 4:6).

I had a non-Christian say to me in apparent earnestness, "Why not have topless women perform at church. It would bring more people in and then you could reach them." But when we have a proper understanding of freedom, we do not seek to promote needed change by pandering to the sinful inclinations of man toward anarchy, licentiousness, or any other fleshly desire. We do not fight abortion by blowing up clinics. Rather we seek to enact change by speaking the liberating truth of Scripture to those in need, by showing the love of Christ in action toward them, and by maintaining a reliance upon the Spirit of God to effect change within them.

AFFECTING PRIVATE TEMPTATIONS

The very personal struggle with temptation and sin is another area in which this enabling freedom engages us. Exercising our freedom in Christ is not an idealistic frolic down Perfection Lane, but it is a hike up Mount Enablement. Being free in Christ does not mean that we shall never struggle with intense and perhaps even prolonged temptation; what it does mean is that we are no longer bound to follow sin's compulsive demands on us. Rather, we are now empowered by His Spirit with the ability to follow a new path, a new course of action.

Over and over again I find myself falling prey to old thoughts or habits that used to lead me directly to sin. Now I can stop and remind myself, "Hey, in Christ I am free from having to let this sin dominate me."

This is not some "positive confession," creating truth out of chaos, but it is positive truth already grounded in the Word of God. But I cannot stop with this understanding; I must press on. I must also see that I am free to let God lead. My obedience is no longer a futile dream, but a living reality based on the fact that God has empowered me with the presence of the Holy Spirit. I am free to let God lead.

A verse I often quote that reminds me where God wants to lead me is Psalm 2:12: "Do homage to [literally "kiss"] the Son, lest He become angry." It thrills me to realize that God is leading me to do what before was unattainable—kiss the Son by my obedient attitude and actions (John 14:21).

I may not always exercise this freedom as I should, which is sin that needs to be confessed and dealt with, but how exciting and liberating to know that in Christ I have the power finally to choose to respond to that person, situation, or sin the way God would have me to. Now that is true liberation, true restoration, and true enablement.

AFFECTING PERSONAL GOALS

One final area in which this empowering freedom affects us is the desire for achievement and accomplishments. All of us, young or old, know the pressures of wanting the respect and admiration of our parents and peers. The tragedy is that some of us have spent our entire lives enslaved to others' approval. We work, drive, and push for that elusive kiss of acceptance. But when we have been set free in Christ, we are no longer restricted to living for the esteem of man.

I'll never forget when God taught me this. I was in the middle of planting a small church when a much larger church contacted me about their pulpit vacancy. The temptation was to seek this position as a means of elevating myself in the eyes of my family and friends.

One "minor" problem stood in my way. I knew it was not God's timing. One day while I was out cutting the grass, still wrestling with this desire for man's approval, God spoke to my heart. He reminded me, "Barry, if you are serving Me, you owe no man an apology. You are free to be what I have called you to be. You are free to do what I have called you to do. You are free to please Me!"

It was one of the most liberating times in my life. In a way

I had never understood before, I knew I was free to be all God wanted me to be. Truly, I owed no man an apology for being happy doing what God wanted me to do and for being where He wanted me to be. Furthermore, in living as He wants now, I will owe Him no apology on the day when each man's work will be made evident (1 Cor. 3:13). The earnest prayer of my life now is that when God calls me home, I'll enter His presence with no apologies for how I spent my life, and I'll hear those liberating words, "Well done, good and faithful servant, enter into the joy of your master."

If right now you are going through life trying to justify your existence by gaining the approval of a parent or a friend, you will spend your life in bondage. You will also ensure that one day when God calls you home, you will owe Him the greatest apology of all. An apology to the One who loved you and offered you the opportunity of a lifetime in freedom.

Yes, freedom in Christ affects my motivation for living. To live for Him is to guarantee no ultimate apologies!

FREEDOM THAT MOTIVATES

In Christ we have entered the fulfilling sphere of freedom. We have been brought out of bondage to sin, restored to an eternal relationship with the Father, and set on a new course of enablement by the ever-present power of the Holy Spirit. It is this freedom alone which provides the proper motivation for changing society, changing my attitude and actions, and changing my reason for living.

What we possess in Christ staggers the imagination. Pardon and freedom are only the beginning. There are yet three more areas of possession in Christ which lay the groundwork for the spiritual life.

three

1 Corinthians:
Sanctification in Christ

In Don Baker's book, *Beyond Rejection,* he tells the moving story of a believer who desperately wanted deliverance from the awful trap of homosexuality but instead kept slipping deeper and deeper into its web.

> *Jerry's homosexual experiences reached a peak while he was preparing for Christian ministry in seminary. The intense academic pressure with the increased spiritual pressure seemed to trigger an even greater and more obsessive need for sexual release.*
>
> *He would spend his days in seminary classrooms and his nights "cruising" the streets of Portland.*
>
> *A confirmed, practicing homosexual, he would walk into any one of the city's many gay bars, sit down at one of the tables, order a glass of beer, and begin "looking over the merchandise. . . ."*
>
> *Often Jerry would park his car on a distant side street . . . and then quickly enter the old four-story hotel that offered nearly every form of homosexual activity a man might desire.*
>
> *He would remove his clothes, wrap himself in a towel, and move from room to room, looking for that perfect partner*

and that ultimate experience.
In all of his years searching for both, however, he found
neither.[1]

Over a period of twenty years he cried out for help. He went from Christian friends to counselors to psychologists—all to no avail. Deep within, he felt change was an impossibility.

Drs. Frank Minirth and Paul Meier spoke of a man who came to their clinic after years of psychological counseling elsewhere. On the first visit, Dr. Minirth told him that he could get better. He was shocked. Dr. Minirth was the first one who had ever offered him the hope of positive change.

Sadly, I think these two stories are representative of many Christians who go through life thinking they are trapped by a web of bad behavior and unhealthy habits. It is as though they have resigned themselves to the enslaving gods of heredity and environment. They need to hear that change is possible, genuinely possible. They can get better. They need to know that something more than a rearranging of the cobwebs is available. They need to know the spider can be crushed.

A proper understanding of our sanctification in Christ offers such a ray of hope. I do not intend to minimize the important roles heredity and environment play in shaping personality, but I want to emphasize the power inherent in our identification in Christ. We need to explore this concept of sanctification to see how it stands as the signature of God on our lives and how God uses it to promote change within us.

THE PREMIUM ON HOLINESS

THE MEANING

The word *sanctification* simply means "being made holy." The Bible uses the term *holy* to refer to such things as the nation Israel, the priest who ministered at the temple, and the city of Jerusalem. In each instance, whatever bore the name *holy* had been set apart by God for God. It had been taken out of ordinary usage and stood uniquely as God's possession. It was an important designation and identification for it represented the true signature of God. After all, there is nothing that God is, does, or possesses which is not wrapped up in this word *holiness.*

THE HALLMARK OF GOD

Holiness is forever seen as the crowning jewel of God, associated more often with His name than any other attribute. It is the attribute most frequently sounded forth by the angels of heaven. Revelation 4:8 records that "day and night they do not cease to say, 'Holy, Holy, Holy, is the Lord God.' " No other attribute is thrice repeated; no other is sung day and night. We should not think of such angelic repetition as tiresome, like some sing-along dragging on a bit too long. Rather, we should think of the word as being spoken by lovers who cannot say it or hear it enough. To be a lover of God is to be a lover of His Holiness. It is this song of His holiness which floods the temple and spills out into every nook and cranny of heaven.

THE HALLMARK OF THE BELIEVER

Arthur Pierson asserted that "salvation is not by character, but it is not independent of character. Heaven is not and cannot be the home of saved souls, if it be not also the abode of sanctified souls. God could have nothing less than a clean house where He lives."[2] As true as this is, we must note that holiness is not only the designation of the believer in heaven; it is also the designation of the believer on earth.

One clear indication of the premium the Father places on the holiness of the believer now is that at the moment of salvation the Father sets us apart in Christ as His special possession. Titus 2:14 states that Christ "gave Himself for us, that He might redeem us from every lawless deed and purify Himself [literally, "in Himself"] a people for His own possession, zealous for good deeds." By being purified in Christ, we have become His special possession.

The word for possession, *periousios,* is what we would term a hapax in Greek grammar. In other words, it is only found in this verse. But this does not mean the word was an unfamiliar one. It actually had a very rich history behind it. It was used to describe the special spoil, which having been gained in battle would be reserved exclusively for the king. In Christ, we have been marked off as the Father's prized possession. This is His view of us. Having been given this status at the inception of our new life in Christ, the direction for how we are to live in the present and what we can anticipate in the future are now set.

Our sanctification comes in three phases: past, present, and future. It is past as it looks at our position in Christ (1 Cor. 1:2). It is present as it involves our progression in Christlikeness (1 Cor. 6:18-20). It is future as it awaits the prospect of our being totally conformed into the image of Christ (1 Cor. 1:5-9).

Most studies focus on the present or future aspects of our sanctification; however, I believe that a firm grasp on our past sanctification sets the stage for change in the present and assurance for the future. The exhortation in 1 Corinthians 6:18-20 to grow in progressive holiness is governed by the foundational awareness of the past work of sanctification on our behalf (6:9-11). Even our future sanctification in heaven is said to have as its guarantee the fact that God has already sanctified us in Christ (1 Cor. 1:5-9).

In fact, Paul could not even complete his greeting to this church without attaching the truth of being in Christ to this theme of sanctification: "To the church of God which is at Corinth, to those who have been sanctified in Christ Jesus, saints by calling, with all who in every place call upon the name of our Lord Jesus Christ" (1:2).

The same idea is conveyed in 1 Corinthians 1:30. There Paul says, "But by His doing you are in Christ Jesus, who *became* to us wisdom from God, and righteousness and sanctification, and redemption" (emphasis added). He *became* (past tense) our sanctification.

These two verses show Paul making a crucial assessment of our spiritual life: at salvation we were instantly identified as holy in Christ. This holiness is not something we must seek after, nor does it come as a second work of grace or as a second-degree sanctification. It is a part of all that we possess from the moment we were placed into Christ.

This foundational truth of our already-accomplished sanctification in Christ becomes the touchstone for change in our lives.

OUR STANDING IN CHRIST

A HOLY IDENTIFICATION

When I lived in Israel, I would occasionally visit Hezekiah's tunnel in the old city of David. The first time, as I made my way through the tunnel from the Gihon Spring to the Pool of Siloam, I was enveloped by such a blackness that I literally could not see my hand directly in front of my face. I had come prepared with some matches and a candle, but they proved no equal to the elements. The wind currents constantly blew out the candle. As a result, I found myself groping slowly through the dark tunnel reminding myself that the next time I was going to bring a flashlight. I knew I needed a light that could alter my dark environment rather than succumb to it.

Spiritually, we need the same. And when God sanctified us in Christ, He gave us what we needed. He set a light within us that all the darkness of sinful habits has proven powerless to extinguish.

Arthur Custance, in his book *Man in Adam and in Christ,* touched on the importance of this positional truth:

> The medieval theologians rightly said, "In Adam a person made human nature sinful; in his posterity nature made persons sinful." This is surely true. But it is also wonderfully true that in the Last Adam, a person made human nature pure; and in His posterity, thenceforth a new nature was to make persons pure.[3]

This is what Christ has done for us.

ADVANTAGES OF OUR POSITION IN CHRIST

When faced with the fatigue of failure, we tend to see little benefit in such positional truth. We want help. What we must realize is that our holy position in Christ provides us with the needed resources. It brings with it decisive advantages.

Our sanctification provides the proper motivation for progressive change.

The only way we are going to uproot a worldly love is to have it supplanted with divine love; our holy position in Christ makes that a reality. Romans 5:5 says, "The love of God has been poured out within our hearts through the Holy Spirit who was given to us." I have heard Christians say, "I can't love this person." Why not? In our own strength such love may be an impossibility, but in Christ, the supplanting love of God has taken root in our hearts. We are not only exhorted to love, but we are properly motivated by the ongoing work of the Holy Spirit.

The only way we are going to forsake a worldly lifestyle is by having it supplanted by a divine lifestyle. Again, our holy position in Christ has secured such a lifestyle for us. First Corinthians 6:18-20 reminds us: "Flee immorality. Every other sin that a man commits is outside the body, but the immoral man sins against his own body. Or do you not know that your body is a temple of the Holy Spirit who is in you, whom you have from God, and that you are not your own? For you have been bought with a price; therefore glorify God in your body."

Some will try to hide behind the excuse that they became Christians too late in life to see God really make much of a dent in their behavior and lifestyles. But God is not a respecter of person or age. If you are in Christ, the active presence and transforming work of the Holy Spirit is guaranteed because at the moment of salvation, you became His temple.

And what a temple it is! The Greeks had two words to describe it. The first was *hieron*. This word described the

whole enclosure of the temple area, including the outer
courts and porticoes. The second word, *naos,* was far more
specific. It described the special dwelling place of God where
His Shekinah glory dwelt: the holy of holies.

It is breathtaking to realize that the word used in 1 Corinthians 6:19 is *naos.* In Christ we have become the very dwelling place of God; therefore, our strength for change and our
motivation toward godliness is intrinsic, not externally im-
posed. He now confronts sin in our lives not on the basis of
what we should become but on the basis of what we are—
holy in Christ.

Our sanctification establishes the guarantee of progressive change.

By His Spirit He lets us see our need for greater purity in our
walk with Him. Then He creates within us the desire for this
kind of walk and provides us with the strength to achieve it.
Most important, He gives us the guarantee that change is
possible based on what we have already become. The Holy
Spirit uses no wands, mirrors, or sleight of hand. He is not
trying to make us become something we are not but rather to
carve into our experience what we are in Christ.

We have not become His temple so that we could become
holy. We have been made holy so as to become a fit dwelling
place for God. This distinction is vitally important. The former puts us in a position of still striving for victory over the
hurdles of our life by our own effort. But, lacking His essential signature, we wonder how long it will be before He
decides to vacate the premises. On the other hand, the latter
position allows us to put our holy status in Christ to work
for us as we build on the relationship God has already firmly
put into place.

In the book, *Beyond Rejection,* Don Baker writes that Jerry
(the man whose story I related at the beginning of this chapter) finally began to experience the power to change which is
inherent in Christ. It took a lot of godly love, care, and
accountability, but change did begin to take place. Later on
as Jerry was growing, Pastor Baker shared with him 1 Corin-

thians 6:11: "And such *were* some of you [homosexuals, v. 9]; but you *were* washed, but you *were* sanctified, but you *were* justified in the name of the Lord Jesus Christ, and in the Spirit of our God (emphasis added)." Jerry responded, "Pastor, why didn't you use 1 Corinthians 6:9-11 [earlier] in our discussions together? I needed the hope."[4] I remember reading that sentence in Baker's book and muttering to myself, "Don't we all, Jerry, don't we all."

We all need to know the decisive advantage of our holy standing in Christ. It is not that our status promotes the perfection of a sinless life on the earth, but it does help us sin less because it allows us to find in Christ the proper motivation and guarantee for daily change.

IMPLICATIONS OF SANCTIFICATION IN CHRIST

BELONGING TO ANOTHER

It is interesting to trace through the New Testament the terms used to designate the followers of Christ. The chart below shows the number of times the terms *disciple* and *saints* are used in the Gospels, Acts, and the epistles. As the chart below indicates, the term *saints* is not used in the Gospels and only four times in the Book of Acts, however, its exclusive usage in the epistles leaves little doubt that *saints* is certainly God's name for us today. The term *saints* has been thrust into the limelight as followers *of* Christ have become followers *in* Christ. We now bear the signature of God. We belong to Him as His unique and special possessions.

	Disciple	Saints
Gospels	230	0
Acts	30	4
Epistles	0	55

As I shared this truth with a young lady whose husband had abandoned her, she began to gather herself and for the first time made eye contact with me and said, "Where does it say I belong to Christ?" Her eyes spoke it all. It was the look of a hope of belonging, a hope of genuine worth. Together we read 1 Corinthians 3:23: "You belong to Christ."

The authors of a recent *Psychology Today* article, "The Healing Brain," believe that individuals with a strong sense of belonging may have minds that are better adapted to preventing disease.[5] Whether or not that bears out remains to be seen, but what is obvious is that God has built within all of us the need to belong. Our problem comes when we try to find someone or something other than the Creator to fill it.

Often our rationale for habitual sin is: "It makes me feel as if I belong." But at what price? Gary Ezzo put it best: "Physical sex, real or otherwise, outside of marriage is but a symptom of a need to know and be known. For whatever reason, we sense a void in our lives and instead of turning inward to self-examination and upward for God's direction, we turn outward to society's solutions."[6]

A secure sense of belonging to God in Christ is the first major step toward disengaging ourselves from the pull of belonging to the world. Our sin nature still abides in us, but we no longer abide in it. The partnership has ended. We belong to another—Christ Jesus our Lord.

One of the key indications of the carnality of the Corinthian church, as recorded in 1 Corinthians 1–4, was their continual dependence on fleshly indicators of their worth and sense of belonging. Paul cut to the quick of all such nonsense when he said all believers first belong to Christ. We bear His name.

OUR USEFULNESS

What God possesses, God uses. There is no such thing as a saint incognito. The term *saint* is only found once in the New Testament.[7] All the other references are plural *(saints)*; and thus carry with them the association of ministry to one another. This is why 1 Corinthians has more to say about serving and the exercise of spiritual gifts than any other book of the Bible. (See 1 Corinthians 11–16.) We have been set apart as saints for saintly service.

When we resist His work in us, 1 Corinthians 3:1-17 shows the tragic consequences: (1) we stunt our spiritual growth, (2) we become useless, and (3) we lose our rewards at the Judgment Seat of Christ. What a poignant reminder that without holiness, we cannot be of any use to Him, regardless of how great our spiritual gifts may be.

Several years ago I was in a car wreck in the early hours of the morning and I was taken to an emergency room. As the doctor walked in, he pointed to surgical instruments lying on a table nearby. He asked a nurse, "Are they sterilized?" She gave the rather hesitant response "Yes—I think so." His next sentence rang with conviction: "Get me instruments I can use!"

Isn't this what God is saying? His basic requirement is that we be clean and available. Today we pass off a lot under the guise of ministry, but a ministry without holiness is an unholy ministry. It lacks the signature of God.

You may be thinking, *If that's the case, I'm washed up; God could never use me. I have blown it too many times.* If you have constantly struggled with sinful habits, you may have a tendency to throw in the towel and resign. Don't. Genuinely and wholeheartedly acknowledge your sin to the Lord and then stand on the truth that you are the unique and special possession of God and vitally useful to Him.

I heard a street preacher say, "What God possesses, He uses because God don't make no junk!" Even Isaiah had to be touched with the burning coals of purification before he could be used. In the life of this prophet, we see the willing compassion of God to cleanse, renew, and use. God showed no reluctance to use Isaiah after he was purified. In fact, the Lord quickly commissioned him into service (Isa. 6). He will do the same for you if you will let Him.

God's desire is that you belong to Him and be fashioned into usefulness for Him. This is why He has sanctified you in Christ.

THE GUARANTEE OF BELONGING TO CHRIST

A lot of marines come through the doors of our church. One of these marines, Glenn, told me about the day an old drinking buddy of his showed up in town and wanted to go cruise the streets. Glenn responded to the invitation by saying, "I'd love to see you but I won't go drinking with you." There was a moment of silence (as if a funeral procession had just passed by), and then his old friend spoke, "Is this the Glenn I used to know?"

"Well, yes and no. I'm still Glenn, but I'm not the same person you used to know." The conversation ended quickly, but Glenn emerged from it with a deeper understanding of his position in Christ.

In your life today, the Holy Spirit engages Himself in prompting you to say "no" to the world and "yes" to God. His work is not external but based on the fact that at the moment of salvation you were sanctified in Christ and became the special dwelling place of God. By belonging to Him, the cobweb has been taken down. More important, the spider has been crushed and the road to change—honest to goodness change—has been paved for you!

four

Ephesians:
Abundant Blessings in Christ

The New Testament has a lot to say about prosperity and riches. In fact, the term *riches* is used 21 times. Surprisingly, we find it mentioned five times within the first three chapters of Ephesians. This should give us a good clue as to what the Book of Ephesians is all about. The people of Ephesus, like many Americans, were well acquainted with wealth and riches. Ephesus was the bank of Asia, and it was the site of the temple of Diana. This temple, one of the seven wonders of the world, served as a repository of wealth and some of the finest art treasures in the ancient world.

The people of Ephesus knew the wealth which comes from man. What was crucial for their spiritual growth was that they come to know the wealth which comes from God. They had to realize the superior quality and spectrum of God's riches as opposed to the transitory and confined riches offered by the world.

It is still true today. We all want to be prosperous Christians, but what are the ingredients of such a Christianity? Much of what is being presented on TV as genuine Christianity suggests that the essential ingredients of a prosperous Christianity are health and wealth. But an emphasis on such ingredients is fraught with spiritual peril.

I had a friend who was terminally ill. In her deathly sickness she was able to lead her daughter-in-law to the Lord and was a tremendous testimony to all those around her. Yet, a few months prior to her death she had some Christians come by for a visit. Like Job's friends, they explained that something must be missing in her faith because she was not experiencing the blessings of divine healing.

When I came to visit her, the spark of contentment and trust were temporarily gone from her eyes. She lay there confused and defeated, beaten down by "spiritual rebuke." I can remember thinking how thankful I was for a book in the Bible which focused on the real ingredients of God's blessings. We began to read carefully through Ephesians. As we noted both the unique quality and spectrum of God's abiding blessings for her, I could see the clarity restored to her thinking and vitality to her spiritual life as she realized that even in a debilitating illness God was not shortchanging her one iota. He was still there. He was still caring. He was still blessing.

Never have people been in greater need of hearing this message than we are today.

THE UNIQUE QUALITY OF GOD'S BLESSINGS FOR US

SPIRITUAL IN NATURE

A friend I was trying to witness to came to see me a couple of days after he had watched a game show on TV. He was disturbed. At the beginning of the show a contestant had introduced herself as a Christian. By the end of the show, she had lost badly. My friend asked, "Why didn't God let her win?"

His question leads us to the issue of what constitutes the real blessings of God. God does bless materially, mentally, and medically, but nowadays we are being sold a hybrid Christianity in which these earthly blessings are viewed as the unique and special blessings of God on His children. Jesus, however, taught just the opposite. The rain falls on the just and the unjust, and the sun shines on the just and the unjust (Matt. 5:45). The believer does not have dibs on such blessings. They are found equally among the lost and the saved.

Furthermore, what may be termed the "earthly blessings" of wealth and health have turned into curses for some. I have read of more than one lottery winner who says that money ruined his life.

Even the blessing of a long life may slowly deteriorate into nothing short of misery. A lady once confided to me that she thought she must have done something wrong to warrant the curse of old age when she wanted to go home to heaven. The great Scottish preacher Samuel Rutherford said at the end of his life as he lay diseased with a fever for over thirteen weeks, "I bless my God that there is a death and a heaven; . . ."[1]

Therefore, an honest analysis of the blessings of health and wealth show that they are for the saved and the unsaved, and that oftentimes they end up not being what they were cracked up to be. This should send home a message loud and clear: we are all too often very poor judges of what really constitutes blessings in our lives. What we *think* are God's greatest blessings can prove to be unstable and transitory.

If we do not grapple with these limitations of earthly blessings, our view of God and His true riches will become grossly distorted. One Christian teacher has a novel interpretation, which he claims was given to him by the Lord, of Jesus' challenge to the rich young man to give away everything and follow Him (Mark 10:17-23). This teacher feels the man was rich to begin with because he had been following the Jewish law and he would have become richer by giving to the Lord: "This was the biggest financial deal that young man had ever been offered, but he walked away from it because he didn't know God's system of finances."[2]

This interpretation is not even close to what Jesus is actually saying in this passage. In fact, it borders on obliterating the real riches of God. A careful perusal of the passage shows that Jesus does speak about treasure, but it is "treasure in heaven" (v. 21). Also, Jesus was answering the question of what the man lacked for salvation, not in what stocks he should invest (v. 17). What the rich young man lacked was a willingness to commit himself totally to Christ. Finally, Jesus concludes by telling His disciples how hard it will be for the wealthy to enter the kingdom of God because they will not put Him first (v. 23).

We would do well to remember G.K. Chesterton's admonition that "those who worship health cannot remain healthy,"[3] and add to it that those who worship wealth cannot remain wealthy. We must be willing to give it all up to follow Him.

God does bless financially, mentally, and physically; but when God wants to truly and uniquely bless, He blesses spiritually. It is God "who has blessed us with every spiritual blessing in the heavenly places in Christ" (Eph. 1:3). Earthly blessings come and go. They may be viewed alternatively as blessings or curses. But the real and lasting blessings of life are spiritual. These spiritual blessings are reserved only for the believer and do not ebb and flow with the tide of human emotions or fluctuating circumstances. They will never fade or change. They will forever remain the best that God can give.

HOUSED IN CHRIST

God has withheld nothing for your benefit. When God identified you in His Son, He not only smashed the gates of hell, but He also threw open the vaults of heaven.

He has earmarked spiritual blessings for you in Christ. Without a doubt, this is the pivotal truth for understanding the entire Book of Ephesians: the concept is mentioned at least forty times in a span of only 155 verses. The unfathomable riches of Christ (3:6-8) and every spiritual blessing in the heavenly places (1:3) are but two of the special benefits we are given in Christ.

You will not find a few of God's spiritual blessings in Christianity and a few more in Islam, Buddhism, Hinduism, or other religions. Absolutely no spiritual riches of God exist outside of Christ. None. They have all been constructed from the hardwood of the Cross, and they become your possession the moment you yield your life to Christ. It is this inheritance in Christ that alone distinguishes God's blessings to the saved.

THE ARRAY OF GOD'S BLESSINGS FOR US

When we do not focus on the real quality of God's blessings, we begin to "ho-hum" the entire collection. Vance Havner explained that years ago in a certain part of Africa where uncut diamonds were extremely plentiful, a traveler happened to notice two little boys playing marbles in the street. The traveler couldn't help but observe the beautiful glitter of the marbles as they rolled in the dirt. His curiosity got the best of him, so he crossed the street for a closer look. Sure enough, his suspicions were confirmed—these little boys were playing marbles with diamonds.[4] This is what can happen to us if we are not careful. We can get so caught up in the temporal that we treat with contempt the real jewels of God's blessings.

In Ephesians 1:3-14 we are given a most impressive catalog of blessings which will stand the test of time, circumstances, or trials. It is fitting that these twelve verses actually constitute one long sentence of doxological praise. We find Paul launching into this glorious doxology with a majestic contempt for grammar and analysis as he contemplates the foundational blessings which we now possess in Christ.

FOUNDATIONAL BLESSINGS
Chosen and adopted in Christ (Eph. 1:3-6).
We are what we are physically because of our parents, and we are what we are spiritually because of our Heavenly Father. God has compassionately chosen to work in the hearts of undeserving sinners to draw them to Himself. As recorded in Luke 14:15-24, Jesus taught that despite man's resistance, the Father was going to have a family. He would start first in the city and if those in the city would not come, He would send His servants out to the highways and byways. The cities were the place to find people. The fact that God would send

His servants out into the desolate regions where the proba-
bility of finding anyone was greatly diminished shows His
absolute commitment to bringing people into fellowship
with Himself.

What motivated God to design such a plan? Was He fulfilling an inner need? No! Was He merely acting on a whim?
No! He was motivated by His compassionate love for lost
sinners. Dr. Chafer, the founder of Dallas Seminary, states:
"Salvation springs from the love God has for His creatures,
which love can be satisfied by nothing short of their confor-
mity to Christ in His eternal presence."[5] This is why God can
offer salvation to all people regardless of the depth of their
misery and sin—salvation springs not from some uncertain
depth of misery or depravity but from the unsearchable
depths of God's love.

The end result of such love is our adoption as sons and
daughters. But the type of adoption spoken of in the New
Testament is qualitatively different than that which some
American couples experience.

I once counseled a college student who was going through
terrible doubts about his salvation. He felt sure that God was
going to disown him. Then one day we hit on the problem.
He had been adopted after his parents had given up trying to
have children of their own. Then less than two years after his
adoption, they gave birth to a baby boy, followed later by the
birth of a baby girl. Twenty years later he was still convinced
that if they had known the others were going to be born, he
would never have been adopted. This feeling had carried over
into his relationship with his Heavenly Father.

What a revelation for this young man to discover that God
was not ever going to disown him. In fact, God had not only
chosen to adopt him into the family, but He had also given
him the absolute right of sonship with all its privileges and
status. This meant God was not going to bump him for
someone else to come. He would love him no more or no
less than He loves any other child of God.

As unfathomable as it may seem, God loves each of us with
the very same love wherewith He loves the Son. In Jesus'

high priestly prayer before the Father, He prays, "I have made Thy name known to them, and will make it known; that the love wherewith Thou didst love Me may be in them, and I in them" (John 17:26). What a wonderful discovery to realize that the very same love which the Father has toward the Son abides in me and in all other adopted sons and daughters of God! Yes, the very same love. Can you ask for any more than that? This is the blessing of New Testament election and adoption.

Redemption in Christ (Eph. 1:7).

When I was a small boy, my family lived in a tiny community with only a country store nearby. I was always scheming for ways to get my hands on a candy bar (and preferably my mouth, though with three older sisters that was not always a given). One day I carried a $500 bill from a Monopoly game to the store to buy a Milky Way bar. I couldn't understand why the lady would not sell it to me. I had picked the largest bill available. I soon realized that there was only one currency redeemable in the USA.

In heaven there is only one currency by which our redemption from sin may be purchased. It is the blood of Christ. Ephesians 1:7 says, "In Him we have redemption through His blood, the forgiveness of our trespasses, according to the riches of His grace." The Greek actually reads, "We have *the* redemption." In Christ we have the climatic realization of that unique redemption which many down through the ages anticipated and looked for: deliverance from sin and restoration to sonship.

The riches of redemption cannot be obtained any other way but through the blood of Christ. First Peter 1:18-19 reminds us that "you were not redeemed with perishable things like silver or gold from your futile way of life inherited from your forefathers, but with precious blood, as of a lamb unblemished and spotless, the blood of Christ."

A Hindu once said to Canon Holland, "You Christians find God in Christ; we Hindus find Him in ourselves. It is all the same." "With this difference," replied Holland: "real conversions take place through Christ. I can take you to many in this city who will tell you they have found God in Christ." The Hindu replied, "There, you win. I have found none who have found God in themselves."

What a blessing to know the quest is over. God has wooed us back in Christ! We are redeemed.

Inheritance in Christ (Eph. 1:11).

Some things we inherit in life would be better thrown away. We might call them "closet inheritance." Because someone could not bring himself to throw away 300 back issues of *Reader's Digest,* for example, I got to add them to the 300 back issues I could not throw away either.

Other things are of such great value that we would not sell them (even if we could) at any price. Our blessing of inheritance stands preeminent. Ephesians 1:11 says "we have obtained an inheritance" which the Bible goes on to state is "imperishable and undefiled and will not fade away, reserved in heaven for you" (1 Peter 1:4).

In certain cultures you can go into a wealthy man's house where he might politely say, "It is all yours." But you do not demand his wallet, credit card, and checkbook, do you? Of course not; "it is all yours" is only meant figuratively.

In Christ however, there is no such thing. We stand in His train of triumph. We have become "fellow partakers of the promise in Christ Jesus" (Eph. 3:6). We are co-heirs with Christ; and of what is Christ not heir? His riches are unfathomable (3:8); He is head over all things (Col. 1:15-18).

A man came to see me who had lost hundreds of thousands of dollars in the Texas oil industry crash. Approaching retirement, he had little left. Worse still, he was bankrupt spiritually. After a period of time, he made a decision to accept Christ. One day I remarked to him, "Just think—you haven't lost one iota of your inheritance." He looked at me like I was crazy. Then I reminded him that his lasting inheritance was all there, wrapped up in Christ.

Surely, no one in his right mind would care to lose a worldly fortune; but in Christ we can never lose the fortune

God has given us. In Christ, we have the sure, irrevocable promise of inheritance, an inheritance of sharing in all that He is.

Sealed in Christ (Eph. 1:13).

Sealing a document was a common practice in ancient times. It verified that a transaction had been completed, and assured that the document could not be tampered with in the future.

An example of this can be seen from the ancient city of Ugarit, where some sealed cuneiform tablets were discovered in ovens. Ovens may initially seem a strange place to find such tablets, but there was actually a very good reason for them being there. Important documents were written in soft clay. Then the person involved would take his personal seal and make an imprint in the clay. Next, it would be placed in the oven to harden. The oven made firm both the document and the signature, thus providing an irrevocable testimony of the transaction.

God has placed His signature on our hearts (2 Cor. 3:3). He has sealed us in Christ with the Holy Spirit, and the fiery trials of life are the ovens by which His signature becomes firmer and more evident to those around us. Being sealed in Christ by the Spirit is a blessing of everlasting ownership and protection; for what God has signed, Satan can never erase.

Pledge in Christ (Eph. 1:14).

The climax of God's riches is found in Ephesians 1:14. In Christ, the Spirit has been given as a pledge of our inheritance. The Greek term for "pledge," *arrabon,* is used in modern Greek for an engagement ring. The Spirit has been given as our engagement ring and signifies that we belong to Christ.

I knew of a man who placed $10,000 down on a house which he later decided not to buy. He ended up forfeiting his $10,000 deposit. God has given us a pledge, but could He change His mind and forfeit His down payment? The answer is an emphatic NO! His down payment was much too costly. It was not made with perishable gold or silver but with His own Holy Spirit. Rest assured, this is one deposit the Father will never leave unclaimed.

The array of spiritual blessings in Christ is impressive, to say the least. But George MacDonald once warned, "Nothing is so deadening to the divine as an habitual dealing with the outsides of holy things."⁶ We must not only appreciate but also appropriate these blessings for our lives.

RESPONSE TO GOD'S BLESSINGS

PUT THEM TO WORK FOR YOU

William Randolph Hearst had an eye for art treasures from around the world and invested a large fortune collecting them. One day he came across a description of several very valuable items that he thought he simply had to have for his collection. He sent his agent in search of the treasures. Months of effort proved fruitless as he was unable to locate the treasures. Finally, Mr. Hearst was notified that the treasures had been located—in his own warehouse. He had owned them all along but had never used them.

Too often this describes how we approach the blessings of God. When we first look at Ephesians 1:3 which tells us that all these spiritual blessings in Christ are "in the heavenly places," we throw up our hands and say, "Yes, but I want them now!" But the word *places* is not in the Greek. The "heavenlies" is actually referring to the unseen world of spiritual reality in which we live every day.

God's spiritual blessings are not simply designed for the distant future, but they are designed for where we live and do battle daily. He wants us to take these blessings in Christ and apply them to our walk (chaps. 4–5) and warfare (chap. 6) in the Christian life.

As I appropriate these riches in my daily walk, I will begin to walk in a manner pleasing to the Lord (4:1). My life will take on the character of a humble walk (4:2), a pure walk (4:17-24), a love walk (5:2), a light walk (5:8), and a wise walk in dependence on the Spirit of God (5:15-18). If I am truly using my wealth in Christ, then I should be seeing a difference in how I act in the various relationships of my life. I will be more loving and responsive in my marriage (5:22-33) and with my children (6:1-4). I will also exhibit a greater respect and responsibility in the work environment God places me in (6:5-9).

Furthermore, as I appropriate these riches in Christ, I will become strong in the Lord (6:10). The various aspects of God's armor listed in chapter 6 continue to point back to the riches God has established in Christ. You cannot use the armor effectively unless you stand on what you possess in Christ.

The wealth which you have been given in Christ does not make your life comfortable but comforting. It does not make your walk carefree but sturdy. It does not make your struggles easy but triumphant. In short, it determines the quality of your life today.

I do not need $1 million at this precise moment (though I may desire it), but I do need to learn contentment in whatever circumstance I am in (Phil. 4:11). I do not need a great singing voice (though my wife might wish I had one), but I do need speech seasoned with grace (Col. 4:6). I do not need an eruditious mind (though I may dream about it), but I do need to be able to count whatever things were gain to me as loss for the sake of Christ (Phil. 3:7). I do not need a long life (though I would perhaps choose it), but I do need to see that whether I live or die, I am the Lord's (Rom. 14:8). This is the practical fruit which is borne as we draw on our vast riches in Christ.

MAINTAIN PERSPECTIVE

When you dream about that promotion at work, but management selects a non-Christian over you, how does that make you feel about the blessings of God? When you desire a Friday-night date with that special Christian guy or gal, but your best friend gets the call instead, how does that make you react to the blessings of God? When you want a harmonious marriage but your partner walks out on you, how does that make you view the blessings of God?

For some it is a time of real disillusionment, as if God has let them down. But if God should never bless you with another breath or another penny, He has already given you the greatest wealth He has to give, which is found in His Son.

It is not that God is unconcerned about the physical things around us. He cares about every facet of your life. You can cry out to Him for your hurts and needs (1 Peter 5:6-7). The problem comes when you try to turn them into a litmus test of God's special blessings on your life. To make your personal hurts and needs the reference point for determining whether God has or has not blessed you is to guarantee either a life of pride (i.e., "I deserve this") or discontent (i.e., "I deserve better"). In any case, to construct the value of your life on material possessions, power, or prestige is to build an empire which will not last.

We must stick to the one reference point God has given: spiritual blessings in Christ. This gives us the perspective we need, for in Him the true wealth of God's blessings flow.

Ephesus, for a short time, might very well have been the bank of Asia, but its time has come and gone. How comforting to know that in that day when all the earthly banks will foreclose and the stock market makes its final crash, the real treasures of Christ for you will remain what they have always been, never ending and never changing. Such are the blessings of God!

five

Colossians:
Lives of Completeness in Christ

A contemporary political leader often excites crowds by getting them to chant a familiar refrain: "YOU are somebody! You ARE somebody! You are SOMEBODY!" Though it serves as a good rally builder, I cannot help but wonder how many return home, face the same old struggles and hurts, and begin to feel again they are nobodies.

Why does the enthusiasm of such a chant not last more than a few hours? It fails to stick because emotion not based on reality offers no firm foundation, only a temporary elixir for the hurt of man.

Unfortunately, the same trap often ensnares the believer. If our Christianity is nothing more than an emotional refrain, we will find ourselves filing out of churches or conferences and returning home to that same stale air of incompleteness. We will develop a sense of being, not so much dissatisfied with our new life in Christ as much as unsure of its total sufficiency for our lives. We are like many of those at the church at Colossae. They knew Christ was sufficient to save them, but was He sufficient to fulfill their dreams and desires?

We must address this issue of the adequacy of Christ head-on. Is Christ complete? If so, how does His completeness relate to my needs and life?

THE INFINITE REFERENCE POINT

NOT FOUND WITHIN OURSELVES
Jean-Paul Sartre argued that no finite point has any meaning unless it has an infinite reference point. Having read virtually everything he wrote, I find this is one of the few statements of his with which I would agree. In the 1930s, Sartre promised to write an ethic to go along with his philosophy. By the time of his death in 1980, he still hadn't. Perhaps it might be truer to say he never could write such an ethic. Though he saw the need for an infinite reference point, his philosophy was without it.

Dr. John Cionca tells of a young man, John, who though a Christian, sought two major goals to achieve completeness in his life: (1) a job as an emergency medical technician, and (2) to marry Cindy. When he found out he could not become an EMT and that his girlfriend had been dating one of his friends, he committed suicide. "The rug upon which John was standing was a career and his relationship with his girlfriend. His self-esteem, his meaning in life, and his future hope all rested upon the fulfillment of those two desires. When those dreams died, so did John."[1]

I too have had to witness a tragedy—someone who, in light of an incurable disease, was seeking a reason to go on but never found one. Man simply gets weary of believing nice platitudes. A "thought for the day" will never satisfy a life in quest for meaning. If we have no reference point, we are headed for tragedy.

German author Hermann Hesse wrote, "The true profession of a man is to find his way to himself. I have become a writer, but I have not become a human being." Hesse's words are not surprising. The dismal reality is that none of us will find ourselves through accomplishments or self-examination, however noble and exacting the search might be.

The great rallying cry of the humanists has been that we are the captains of our own ship. But what good is it to be the captain of a ship which has no bearings and is destined to sink in forgotten waters?

CHRIST ALONE

A life of wholeness must begin with discovering who or what the infinite reference point is. Jesus warned that this infinite reference point can only be found in Him (Luke 9:24). He is the all-sufficient bearing we need for our lives. "For in Him all the fullness of deity dwells in bodily form" (Col. 2:9). There is absolutely nothing lacking in His person or work.

E. Stanley Jones, in his daily devotional book *In Christ*, speaks of a North Korean refugee living in South Korea who had produced a rather remarkable portrait of Christ. Jones writes:

It has to be seen to be believed. In a space of three feet by four feet of canvas he has written by hand the whole of the New Testament in minute letters in English. There are approximately 185,000 words, with about a thousand words in a line. Out of these words arise a full length figure of Christ. The figure is produced by inking some words more heavily than the others. Out of the words arise the Word. Out of the gospels arises the Gospel. He Himself is the good news.

Around the figure of Christ are twenty-seven little angels, all looking toward Him, some with folded hands in adoration. These twenty-seven little angels represent the twenty-seven books of the New Testament. They are all looking at Him, bringing out the fact that the whole New Testament brings out the Person of Christ—it all looks at Him, the Center.[2]

The fullness of Christ and the general perception.

The world, however, seeks to ameliorate this absolute centrality and distinctiveness of Christ, most often by painting a portrait of Christ as nice and kind but quite inadequate for exclusive worship.

A Gallup poll in the early 1980s gives a startling idea of what most Americans think about Christ. Though 70 percent view Him as more than just another human being, only 42 percent take the orthodox position that He is the incarnate God among men.

AMERICA'S VIEW OF CHRIST

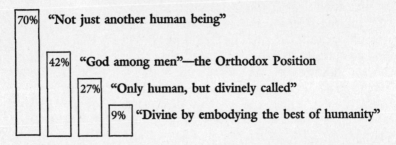

70% "Not just another human being"

42% "God among men"—the Orthodox Position

27% "Only human, but divinely called"

9% "Divine by embodying the best of humanity"

That Christ is less than God has been further reinforced by the film "The Last Temptation of Christ." *Newsweek* labeled the Jesus portrayed as "a very human Christ."[3] With such a perception of Jesus, it is hard to imagine Him bringing completeness to anybody.

Ghandi was not the first (nor will he be the last) to seek to pacify the demands of Christ for absolute worship with admiration and adulation. In fact, legend has it that when Rome caught wind of some of the strange reports emanating from Jerusalem regarding the resurrection of Christ, someone on the senate floor suggested that Jesus be placed alongside the other gods of the Pantheon. Then one senator rose to his feet and asserted, "He does not claim to be a god, but the one and only true God." At which point the discussion ended.

In the interview before the Council on the eve of His crucifixion, Jesus answers affirmatively that He is the Son of the Blessed One and that "you shall see the Son of man SITTING AT THE RIGHT HAND OF POWER, and COMING WITH THE CLOUDS OF HEAVEN" (Mark 14:61-62). Here, Christ unashamedly proclaims a position of absolute power, authority, and completeness. A very human Christ in His sufferings, but a very Divine Christ in His triumph over death.

To pat Christ on the back and say, "Good man!" is nothing but patronizing nonsense. The Bible points to a Christ who demands and commands nothing less than absolute preeminence.

The fullness of Christ and a popular divinity.
The New Age advocates, among others, have also obscured the real distinctiveness of Christ. They feel very comfortable with such terms as "deity" and "fullness." After all, they believe the basic problem of humanity is our inability to awaken to the fact that we are all gods. *Time* magazine reported that someone turned to Shirley MacLaine at one of her seminars and said, "With all due respect, I don't think you are a god." To which she responded: "If you don't see me as God, it's because you don't see yourself as God."[4]

But Christ is not simply a dewdrop of God on the lawn of humanity, nor is He a slice of the cosmic pantheistic pie. He is not one among many, but rather, the One over all. He is the One who holds the keys to death and hell (Rev. 1:18), and contrary to popular belief He has made no duplicates!

He is not, nor was he ever, a "god in the making"; but rather, the God who makes all things! (Col. 1:16-17) Note the preeminent "all-ness" of Christ in Colossians 1–2.

Col. 1:16	For by Him *all* things were created
Col. 1:17	And He is before *all* things
Col. 1:17	And in Him *all* things hold together
Col. 1:19	For it was the Father's good pleasure for *all* the fullness to dwell in Him
Col. 1:20	[For it was the Father's good pleasure] through Him to reconcile *all* things to Himself
Col. 2:3	In whom [Christ] are hidden *all* the treasures of wisdom and knowledge
Col. 2:9	In Him *all* the fullness of Deity dwells in bodily form
Col. 2:10	He is the head over *all* rule and authority

Christ is the Creator and Sustainer of this universe (1:16-17); the Redeemer, Keeper, and Ruler of all things (1:20; 2:3, 10). Simply put, the fullness of God dwells in Him (Col. 1:19; 2:9). The sum total of all the divine attributes belong to Christ. There is absolutely nothing lacking in His person or His work. He is completeness personified. As one theologian stated, "It is vain to seek it [the Godhead] wholly or partially outside of Him."[5]

Without Christ there would be no universe. Without Christ there would be no Gospel. Without Christ there would be no infinite reference point for our lives. D. Martyn Lloyd-Jones, one of the outstanding preachers of the twentieth century until his death in 1981, reminds us that "anything which claims to be Christianity without having Christ as the beginning and the centre and the end is a denial of Christianity, call it what you will. There is no Christianity apart from Him; He is everything."[6]

THE INTERSECTION

STANDING IN COMPLETENESS

We enter a state of completeness only as we enter into a relationship with Christ. Here we come to that cherished phrase "in Christ." It is used at least twenty times in this short letter. It can best be summed up in Colossians 2:9-10: "For in Him all the fulness of Deity dwells in bodily form, and in Him you have been made complete, and He is the head over all rule and authority."

Two important things stand out in these verses. The first is that the word translated "fullness" in verse 9 and the word translated "complete" in verse 10 actually come from the same Greek root, *plēroō*. This establishes the intersection we need. The fact that Christ is God and, therefore, complete in Himself, guarantees that when a person is identified in Him, he is brought into a life of completeness. Christ's completeness alone resolves the incompleteness within man.

Second, our "completeness in Christ" in Colossians 2:10 is viewed as an act already accomplished. When my little boy was born, I was not looking for his ability to quote Shakespeare, but for fingers and toes. In other words, I was not looking for maturity but for completeness. This is what believers have been given in Christ. When you came to Christ, you were not short-changed one iota. God granted you everything pertaining to life and godliness in Christ (2 Peter 1:3).

It is time Christians weigh carefully what Colossians presents about Christ and the completeness He brings. Everything revolves around something. The smallest atomic particles revolve around a nucleus. Our planets revolve around the sun, and our sun revolves around the nucleus of the Milky Way. Everything in life revolves around something else. Colossians maps out that Christ is the center of the universe and human history. Only in Him do we find the missing reference point for our lives. His completeness assures us that we will never have to go outside of Him for anything. Apart from Him we stand alone without bearing. In Him we stand as whole integers.

GROWING IN COMPLETENESS

Maturity could be defined as the art of refining what is already present. A man who is immature, therefore, has done a poor job of sculpturing the direction of his life. In the same way we are complete in Christ at our new birth, but this does not preclude the necessity of maturity.

I mentioned earlier that at the birth of my son I was looking for completeness, not maturity. It is no contradiction, however, to desire to see developmental growth as time goes on, for it is important that a child grow and mature. When a child does not grow, we call it a tragic case of retardation. When a believer does not grow, we call it a tragic case of carnality. Carnality robs us of the rich, daily developmental growth in completeness. Therefore, the strong exhortations in Colossians 1:28 and 2:6 spur us on to developing the muscle and tone reflective of our completeness in Christ.

The truth of the matter is that this is easier said than done. So few of us are exercising the completeness we possess in Christ. It is disturbing to read of the growing number of cases of adultery and abuse within Christian homes. Certainly even the best Christian marriages can go sour and a spirit of incompleteness rear its ugly head anywhere at anytime. How then can we exercise our completeness in Christ? Colossians 3 gives us some clear direction.

Put on.

We are commanded to put on a Christlike heart (Col. 3:12). A heart frozen by bitterness, impatience, disappointment, resentment, and unforgiveness can be warmed as we put on a heart of Christlikeness.

Furthermore, we are to gird our hearts with a belt of love. This belt of love is important because it gives shape and support to the heart. It keeps us from saying, "I'll be patient but I don't want to!" Could you imagine the Lord ever exercising a heart of forgiveness without the belt of love? Christ would never say, "I'll forgive you, but I don't want to." Neither should we. Daily we must check to see if we are wearing the Designer's label—the wardrobe of Christlikeness.

Dwell in.

We are to let the Word of God dwell in us richly (Col. 3:16). For His Word to dwell in us richly is not simply to be a walking Bible encyclopedia or the premiere champion of Bible trivia. For something to dwell in us involves a sense of at-homeness.

One night my wife called me into the kitchen all in a panic. She exclaimed, "There's a snake on the hot water heater!" I went into the kitchen thinking that one of the guests that night had left a toy snake as a joke. Unfortunately it was no joke. There warming itself was a four-to-five-foot snake. Though the snake was in my house, I was not in any way at home with it!

For us to become at home with the Word of God, we must allow the Spirit to make it personal and applicable. We must enjoy its presence in our lives as the Spirit uses it to convict and direct us. The wardrobe of Christlikeness we are to put on is washed, renewed, and kept fresh daily by the ongoing presence of Christ through His Word (Col. 3:15-17).

Lock into.

Colossians 3:1-4 could best be summed up with the phrase "Lock into." We will be able to put on Christlikeness and be at home with the instruction of God's Word as we seek out and lock into the things above.

The rationale for seeking the things above is very clear: This is where our life is now located (Col. 3:3). We must lock in on this heavenly frequency which has been provided for us in Christ. A friend of mine had an alarm clock that seemed to have a mind of its own. Often it would lock in on the wrong frequency and go off at bizarre times. One spring Saturday morning the clock went off at 5 A.M. He reached over and grabbed it, and without ever getting out of his bed, hurled it out the third-story window of his dormitory to the ground. He had had enough of it locking in on the wrong frequency.

We should be so ruthless spiritually. We simply cannot afford to be attached to the discordant sounds of this world. As sheep lock in on their master's voice, so we should have our lives progressively sensitized to the sound and movement of Christ.

What's more, this passage teaches us that we must constantly be ready to reset our lives when we feel a subtle shift along the dial of Christlikeness. We must "keep seeking the things above" (Col. 3:1). This involves a moment-by-moment monitoring of who or what we are tuned to.

When my wife and I went to the Urbana Conference in 1984, participants performed what is called an "attitude check." For example, you are in a line waiting and someone yells out, "Attitude check." Everyone responds, "Praise the Lord!" Since there were over 18,000 people at Urbana and the lines were normally very long, it was a good idea.

As the week wore on with longer waits and nastier weather, the Richter-scale response of those in the lines to "attitude checks" dwindled to a cool ripple. On the last night Kim and I waited outside the coliseum in the freezing rain with hundreds of others, all praying for a bus that was about an hour late. Some conferee, seemingly oblivious to the weather conditions and the mood of those around him, shouted out, "Attitude check." I think he barely escaped with his life.

But in reality, he was right. It is always easy to check my attitude when I know I am on frequency. But I really need to check it when cold winds are chilling my heart and casting aspersions on my completeness.

Growing in completeness means I lock in on those things that engender completeness in Christ, and I ruthlessly discard those things that do not. It also involves becoming more sensitive to honestly evaluate and deal with my attitude, particularly when I find it out of tune with Christ.

THE INCENTIVES OF COMPLETENESS

IT GIVES MEANING TO THE EVERYDAY

All of us have dreams of places we would like to go, things we would like to see, and jobs we would like to complete. Probably very few Christians have not thought, "Lord, I'd prefer the Rapture to come after my wedding day."

But what happens if our days are cut short, or we end up penniless, or if by sickness or misfortune all our aspirations do not come true? A young man I know faces just such a future. One year in high school he was healthy and active. The next year he was struck with cancer and is dying. What does completeness in Christ say to him and the many like him?

It says to them, "You are still complete." Not that works and dreams do not matter, because they do—only for different reasons now. They flow from fullness and not as the world suggests as an attempt to gain fullness. Though the streams of our lives may not have flowed as far or as smoothly as we would have liked, the fount remains the same.

Life flowing from completeness rather than to it is the balm for shattered lives and threatening skies. It gives my life the bearing it needs. The world's measurements for completeness are too small and inadequate to handle all the fragile contingencies of life. In C.S. Lewis' classic *Mere Christianity*. The author's summation is, "Look for yourself, and you will find in the long-run only hatred, despair, rage, ruin, and decay. But look for Christ and you will find Him, and with Him everything else thrown in."[7] When everything is said and done, there is only one who misses out on completeness—it is the one who has missed Jesus Christ.

IT IS A WEAPON AGAINST TEMPTATION

In Colossians 2:11-23 we find that our completeness in Christ provides a powerful weapon against temptation. Most temptation is a promise of fulfillment either physically, mentally, or emotionally. It may bring temporary relief or satisfaction, but never fulfillment. From Eve onward this has been the case. Hebrews 11:25 speaks of the passing pleasures of sin. Some well-meaning Christians talk about sin as if there were no pleasure in it, which is absurd. What is true, however, is that its pleasures are always passing.

Some of us remember Keith Thibodeaux as Little Ricky from the TV series "I Love Lucy." In a recent interview he talked about growing up and seeking meaning in the pleasures of this world. "I'd do so much stuff that sin wasn't really sin to me, it was a pleasure to experience." But eventually he began to see it all turning to emptiness, and he said, "I had gotten to the point where the pleasure of sin had taken its toll on me. The Bible says there is pleasure in sin for a season, but that's it. And I was at the end of my season."[8] What a poignant reminder: if what we are pursuing in life can pass away, it cannot ultimately fulfill. One day the season will end.

Satan may tell us that it is precisely the one thing God has said we cannot have or do not need which will fulfill us. But the truth which disarms his lies is that in Christ "you have been made complete and He is the head over all rule and authority." Everything outside of Christ has no profit, no life, no purpose for being and stores only the wreckage of broken promises and unfulfilled expectations. The only relationship that remains is the one found in Christ. The purpose of God is that all things that continue shall find their meaning and significance in Christ the infinite reference point.

BRINGING THE FRAGMENTS TOGETHER

A little boy told his father that for the grand prize of a banana split, he could put together a rather sophisticated puzzle. The puzzle was a map of the world, and since his father knew his son had only a limited understanding of geography under his belt, he felt safe in going along with the friendly wager. Well, the little boy went to work on it and within an hour had emerged from his room proudly showing the map to his amazed father.

"How could you do that?" his father asked.

The little boy flipped the puzzle over and there on the other side was a beautiful picture of Christ. "It was easy," he said. "Once you get Jesus in the proper place, everything else comes together."

How absolutely true. Do not let the neo-gnostics of our day sell you on a Jesus who is feeble, weak, and wholly incomplete. "For in Him all the fulness of Deity dwells in bodily form, and in Him you have been made complete, and He is the head over all rule and authority" (Col. 2:9-10). Stand against the cacophony of voices by the power of His completeness and find in Him the only lasting basis for meaning and fulfillment in your life. For this is what we have been given in Christ.

Pursuing a New Lifestyle

To be in Christ and allow ourselves to be governed by a worldly lifestyle is to place ourselves in a state of disorientation. Somehow we have got to come to grips with the reality that our possessions in Christ do not merely offer but actually call for and provide for a new way of living. Our identification in Christ can no longer allow us to live the same way we did before we were saved. It is only natural that what captures the heart must move the will. A person possessed by God in Christ will naturally pursue Christlikeness.

This section not only shows that our pursuit of Christlikeness involves the nuts and bolts of day-to-day living, but it also focuses on some very practical ways in which we may continue in our development of a Christlike lifestyle. As we cultivate a lifestyle of Christlike forgiveness toward others, we are highlighting the forgiveness we have received in Christ. As we cultivate a lifestyle of Christlike joy in the midst of daily living, we display the reality of a life in Christ which overcomes the world. As we cultivate a lifestyle of Christlike integrity, we demonstrate to others the soundness with which God changes a life in Christ. Lastly, as we cultivate a lifestyle of Christlike perserverance and victory in our service for Christ, we elevate ministry beyond worldly criteria and develop an understanding of the rewards believers accrue from doing God's will.

six

Philemon:
The Accountability of Forgiveness in Christ

During WW II a Nazi soldier had participated in locking Jewish family members in their house and setting it on fire. He and his fellow soldiers were told to shoot anyone who tried to escape. The horrid memories of seeing some family members aflame by the windows continued to haunt him throughout the war. Then one day he was mortally wounded. Dying in the hospital he asked for a Jew to come visit him. When Simon Wiesenthal came, the soldier begged him for forgiveness for the atrocities he had done. Wiesenthal walked away to let him die in his misery.[1]

What would you have done if the soldier had attacked and killed your family? Perhaps you have been abused in the past, or are right now going through a terrible injustice. In the midst of it all, where does the term *forgiveness* fit into your vocabulary? Many do not quibble over the role of forgiveness when it concerns the spilled-milk episodes of life. But what role does it play when the hurts are deep and the wrongs are evil?

It is here that we must grapple with forgiveness. We cannot treat it as nothing more than a mild insulator to light bruises and minor irritations. This phenomenon called Christian forgiveness must have something to say even from within the caldron of deep pain and overt evil.

THE DEPTH OF FORGIVENESS

Peter came to Jesus with a question: How many times should we forgive someone—seven times? (Matt. 18:21) He knew the rabbinic sayings taught to extend the open hand of forgiveness three times but no more. Therefore, Peter's willingness to increase forgiveness up to seven times must be viewed, I believe, as an indication of this young disciple's heart. He genuinely desired to be a forgiving person

SEVENTY TIMES SEVEN

But Peter's kind gesture was met with a surprising response. Jesus changed the rules concerning the nature of forgiveness by making a quantum shift from the quantitative aspect of forgiveness to the qualitative. He strikes at the heart of unforgiveness when He says to forgive "seventy times seven" (Matt. 18:22). In doing so He forces Peter to wrestle with the real question—*How deep (not how often) will my forgiveness extend?*

Jesus continued to press the issue with the Parable of the Unmerciful Servant (Matt. 18:23-35). The king was willing to write off a debt so high his servant could never pay it back though he were to serve day and night for the rest of his life. However, the servant turned around and would not forgive a peer who owed but a trifling sum in comparison. The story has nothing to do with the amount of times one is to forgive—seven, seventy, or seventy times seven; nor with the degree of the injury or wrong. Rather, it illustrates the depth to which the king was willing to extend mercy, in contrast to the depth to which the servant was willing to exact payment. The lens of this parable focuses sharply on forgiveness as an issue relating to the depth of one's heart, not to the amount or degree of the wrong.

THE DEPTH MANIFESTED IN CHRIST

The quality of forgiveness that is to govern our lives is expressed succinctly in Ephesians 4:32: "And be kind to one another, tender-hearted, forgiving each other, just as God in

Christ also has forgiven you." The depth of forgiveness we are to exercise is none other than the depth of forgiveness we have received in Christ. As C.I. Scofield stated in his reference notes, "Human forgiveness rests upon and results from the divine forgiveness."

This quality of forgiveness does away with the pseudo-forgiveness of "I'll forgive but not forget." Such a forgiveness can never survive in Christ. How fortunate we are that it has not survived with the Father toward us; similarly, it must not be allowed to live among us His children as we interact. Who would like to face the Father and hear Him say, "I'll forgive but not forget"? Within the covenant God has made with us He states, "For I will be merciful to their iniquities, and I will remember their sins no more" (Heb. 8:12). Here we possess the promise of God's forgiving and forgetting.

But what does it mean for God to forgive our sins? Surely there is no lapse of memory in an omnisicient God, is there? Of course not; for God to forget means that He chooses never to relate to us in the future based on past failures. Instead He relates to us based on our beloved position in Christ. The debt will never be thrown back in our faces because it has been permanently nailed to the Cross (Col. 2:13-14). This is the power of forgiveness in Christ displayed in the heart of God. This is the same perspective we are to have toward one another.

Charles "Tex" Watson is one of the people who killed for Charles Manson. He came to know the Lord in 1975. Recently he explained that he had his most important lesson in the meaning of forgiveness in mid-1987. He had begun corresponding with a woman named Suzan Rae LaBerge, from New Mexico. LaBerge wrote to him after hearing his testimony on a Christian radio station. Their long-distance acquaintance grew through more letters, culminating with LaBerge requesting a visit. Watson recalls:

> *We talked for about 30 minutes before the conversation turned toward me. For some reason, she wanted to hear my testimony face-to-face, although she made it clear I did not*

have to talk about my crime if I didn't want to. . . .

But as we shared back and forth, I was still curious about why she would want to visit me. Then the shock came. Suzan said, "I did not know when I came here if I was going to tell you this or not, but I have something to tell you." I thought, Oh, Lord, what's this about? She said, "Rosemary LaBianca was my mother, and I want you to know I forgive you."

I could not believe what was happening. I spent the next half hour filling her full of questions only she could answer. I finally realized who she was and that I had killed her mother and stepfather—Leno and Rosemary LaBianca. . . .

I had experienced the physical act of forgiveness. At the end of the visit, we prayed together, realizing a miracle had just taken place.[2]

When we forgive and forget in Christ, we too engage in the activity of "settling accounts" (Matt. 18:23) of sin by choosing to no longer hold them against the person who has clearly and perhaps quite deeply injured us. We must take our cue from nothing less than the grace of God offered us at the Cross. At the Cross we learn how to receive forgiveness and release from a debt we could never pay; and from its vantage point we must learn how to dispense forgiveness to others. Nowhere but at the Cross do we learn the depth of forgiveness.

THE UNBREAKABLE BOND OF FORGIVENESS AND FELLOWSHIP

Too often we see forgiveness as something God has obligated Himself to give in Christ, but not as something we must necessarily enter into with one another. Queen Elizabeth I once said to the Countess of Nottingham, "God may forgive you, but I never will."

It is amazing how we can engage in "selected senility" for most of our lives. We can forget appointments, names, or car keys, but never the wrongs done to us. But as Paul points out, we can no longer afford such an indulgence. We must apply the depth of forgiveness to the fellowship we have in Christ. The Book of Philemon forms what we might call a holy triad: the constant interplay between being in Christ, harmonious fellowship, and exercising deep forgiveness. It is obvious that both the forgiveness and the fellowship spring from union in Christ. How they in turn relate to one another is crucial for our spiritual growth and the nurturing of the body as a whole.

FORGIVENESS DEEPENS FELLOWSHIP

True forgiveness always brings authenticity to fellowship, both with God and with one another. In the model prayer given by Christ there is an undeniable link between forgiveness and fellowship: "And forgive us our debts, as we also have forgiven our debtors" (Matt. 6:12).

What is Christ saying here? Certainly there is no fickleness within the character of God. He is not playing a wait-and-see game with us of "I'll forgive you if you'll forgive others." The issue here is not objective forgiveness (justification) in Christ, but daily growth and fellowship with the Father. Hence, the aspect of daily forgiveness towards one another can be said to directly affect the daily fellowship we may enjoy with the Father. "It is impossible for one to be in fellowship with God as long as he harbors ill will in his heart."[3]

This nurturing of forgiveness in Christ also promotes genuine fellowship with one another because we begin to interact with the same compassion, mercy, and forgiveness which has been extended to us. As George Herbert points out, "He that cannot forgive others breaks the bridge over which he himself must pass if he would ever reach heaven; for everyone has need to be forgiven."[4]

Forgiveness toward one another is not an option. It establishes the tone and depth of fellowship both with the Father and with His people.

FELLOWSHIP DEEPENS FORGIVENESS

Paul addresses the flip side of this coin when he looks at the effect of fellowship on forgiveness in Philemon 4-6: "I thank

my God always, making mention of you in my prayers, because I hear of your love, and of the faith which you have
toward the Lord Jesus, and toward all the saints; and I pray
that the fellowship of your faith may become effective
through the knowledge of every good thing which is in you
for Christ's sake." Their fellowship was alive because it was
centered in Christ and, as such, it made a difference in how
they related to one another. This reciprocity is clearly established in verse 5 with the repetition of the preposition *toward*. Actually the Greek text here uses two different preposi-
tions. The first is *pros* which is normally translated "toward."
The second, however, is *eis* which is most commonly translated "into," and carries with it the idea of making contact. The
distinction is important. If we are to direct our love and faith
toward the Lord Jesus, we must take close aim at the believers around us. The "contact" is made with them. If our fellowship is truly in Christ, then our love for Christ will express itself in how we relate, not to a select few, but to all the
saints.

This certainly does not mean that we forgive only believers, but it does point us to the starting gate. We are merely
whistling in the dark if we think we can love a lost world for
Christ when we cannot even love the brethren for whom
Christ died and to whom we stand united. Furthermore, a
hatred toward the brethren is said to be a clear indication
that we do not possess the love of the Father within us
(1 John 4:20-21).

This is the harsh reality of a false and flimsy fellowship. A
lack of genuine forgiveness in the church shows the poor aim
of our love and faith toward Christ. I believe it is one of the
primary reasons that the church is so anemic today.

While I was studying at Hebrew University in Israel, several of the other believers and I banded together to have a
Bible study in my dorm room. We felt we needed the fellowship, and we also wanted to be a testimony to others in the
college community. It was a time of positive outreach, but
we did have our struggles. In fact, the wide diversity of
backgrounds within the group presented enough problems to

cause most groups to splinter off into oblivion. But, instead of quitting or splitting, we became more cohesive as the year went on—for one simple reason: we had nowhere else to go but to each other. It wasn't possible to pack up our Bible, sneakers, take our fellowship ball, and go play Christianity elsewhere. We were all we had and we knew we needed each other.

Furthermore, we knew unbelievers around us needed a real demonstration of the love of Christ as we ourselves "made contact" with one another. This bottom-line desire to model the forgiveness of God in Christ overrode the petty personality conflicts of day-to-day living. To hear comments like "I'm sorry"; "I know we disagree, but thanks for listening"; or "I'll still stand beside you" was so edifying and unifying; they were precious links in the chain of fellowship. It should come as no surprise that at the end of the year, there was a sense of sadness in saying good-bye. I left Israel with more than a broader knowledge of the land, language, and customs. I had become aware of the interrelationship between forgiveness and fellowship in Christ. Our fellowship in Christ had deepened within us a responsibility of forgiveness, which in turn had strengthened our fellowship. And through it all, God allowed us to leave behind a testimony of Christlike love to an observing community.

How sad that the church in America knows little of the interaction between forgiveness and fellowship in Christ. How can it when the tendency is to jump from steeple to steeple over issues that have nothing to do with doctrine? You will never tap the riches of fellowship until you are willing to prime the pump with Christlike love and forgiveness.

THE OUTWORKING OF FORGIVENESS

An awareness that fellowship in Christ necessitates a forgiving spirit leads us to the threshold of responsibility. The particular obligations enjoined on both the guilty and the innocent parties are addressed in Philemon 7-21.

RESPONSIBILITIES OF THE GUILTY
Onesimus was a runaway slave hiding in Rome. He had apparently stolen from his master Philemon to make the journey (v. 18). Some time after arriving in Rome, he came into contact with Paul and was converted (v. 10).

There Onesimus faced the most difficult decision of his young Christian life—whether or not to go back to Philemon. If he chose to return, the prospects were bleak. He had no money or resources to pay back what he had stolen. What's more, the penalty for a runaway slave was severe. There were an estimated 60 million slaves in the Roman Empire at the time. To discourage revolt, Roman law gave slaveowners like Philemon the widest latitude to do with runaway slaves as they willed. In fact, from a legal standpoint, the best that Onesimus could hope for was that an "F" (Latin for *fugitivus*) would be branded on his forehead with a hot iron. The worst prospect, though, was death by crucifixion.[5]

Do not use Christianity to hide wrong.
So why go back? If Onesimus were living today, he might be advised by many in the church to claim 1 John 1:9 ("If we confess our sins, He is faithful and righteous to forgive us our sins and to cleanse us from all unrighteousness"), dismiss the sin as in the past, and do nothing to make the wrong right.

The idea of restitution or the simple acknowledgment of wrong seems almost passé in our day and time. I have a friend who shared with me how his brother-in-law divorced my friend's sister to marry my friend's wife. You almost have to draw diagrams to make heads or tails of this tangled mess of sin. While this took place almost ten years ago, the tragic repercussions have continued to reverberate. Not long ago, my friend wrote asking if there might be a sense of genuine forgiveness and restoration between the two families. He received a letter back in which the man, who is now a "prosperity pastor," categorically rejected the notion that he needed to ask anyone for forgiveness. Hiding behind 1 John 1:9, he claimed that he had been forgiven by God for whatever things he may have done, and never needed to concern himself with those he had hurt.

But to take 1 John 1:9 and gallop in the fields of sin unencumbered is to ride in the saddle of heresy. First John 1:9 is a contract of restoration, never a license to sin. When it is applied correctly, it is a source of immeasurable comfort. To soothe a soul burdened by sin with the promise of a faithful God who cleanses and restores to fellowship is one thing; to use this verse as a carte blanche for sin is quite another. We simply cannot step over people while waving the banner of 1 John 1:9 and expect to get closer to God. The moment we began to abuse this verse as an excuse to sin or to dismiss the hurt we have caused others, we are headed for spiritual downfall.

Onesimus would have nothing to do with hiding behind the freedom of Christianity. He knew that his faith would be a substanceless shell if it entitled believers to default on their debts toward one another, or if it promoted within believers a cavalier approach to the wrongs or hurts inflicted on others.

Recognize the blessings that await you.

The child of God can ill afford to use such smoke screens for seeking and granting forgiveness. The blessings of daily fellowship with God rest on meeting the moral obligation to address the injuries we have caused others (Matt. 6:18). Our spiritual and mental health demands it.

In college, I felt the need to go back to one of my former teachers and apologize for my behavior and attitude toward him. I knew he would think I was crazy. I supposed that he would probably not even recall the specific incidence. But I also knew that God wanted me to correct the wrong, and that was what mattered most. I think I know how Onesimus must have felt as he drew closer to Philemon's house, carrying Paul's letter in his hand. I approached this teacher's door with fear and trembling; but I left there soaring on the wings of freedom. It was as if a heavy weight had been removed from me. A renewed sense of refreshment and fellowship with God was born from that one simple act of obedience.

However, our willingness to right the wrong does not guarantee that we will always be met with a favorable response. Onesimus, after all, had no such guarantee, and neither do we. But standing at that teacher's door showed me that the peace of God far exceeds whatever cost might be incurred to rectify the wrong. I can live without whatever money I must forfeit. I can live without whatever status in society I must forfeit. I can even live without their willingness to forgive; but as a Christian I cannot live without the peace of God on my life.

This does not mean that we should go looking for dirty laundry to stir up. It does mean, however, that if God convicts us as to our need to act, we must not dive under 1 John 1:9 for cover.

The question for Onesimus was no longer, *Why go back?* Rather it was, *How could I not go back?* It is axiomatic. One who gets right with God cannot rest till he does what he can to make it right with his fellowman. What was true of Matthew and Zaccheus as tax-gatherers, and of Onesimus as a runaway slave, is true for you and me today. W. Graham Scroggie, whose pastorates included Spurgeon's tabernacle in London, summed it up accurately: "One of the surest evidences of the presence of grace in the heart is the resumption of neglected duties; a return to the things from which we have run away."[6] Stop your running and experience the peace of full reconciliation.

RESPONSIBILITIES OF THE INJURED PARTY
Philemon had suffered a great loss by the defection of Onesimus. Paul does not approach him on legal grounds; he knew Philemon's rights. Instead, Paul asks him to focus on the preeminently better ground of union in Christ.

Maintain a proper viewpoint of the guilty party.
Paul could have exhorted Philemon to forgive Onesimus with a variety of arguments. He chose one, though: the bond in Christ. Onesimus would now live up to his name (which

in the Greek means "profitable") because he has not only returned to Philemon in the flesh but also "in the Lord" (v. 16). Paul goes on to say, "If then you regard me a partner, accept him as you would me. . . . Yes, brother, let me benefit [Greek verbal form of *Onesimus*] from you in the Lord; refresh my heart in Christ" (vv. 17, 20).

With this play on words, Paul weaves the thread of forgiveness throughout the tapestry of our fellowship in Christ. "In Christ" carries in it the secret of all sweet humanities and beneficences; it is the spell which calls out fairest charity and is the only victorious antagonist of harshness and selfishness."[7] Paul places the spiritual status of Onesimus ahead of all else. He did not request that Philemon simply receive Onesimus back as a returned slave, or as a returned brother, but as a beloved brother in Christ (v. 16).

All other distinctions become irrelevant. "There is neither Jew nor Greek, there is neither slave nor free man, there is neither male or female; for you are all one in Christ Jesus " (Gal. 3:28). Scroggie acknowledged, "Christianity recognizes the fact of social distinctions, but does away with the tyranny and offensiveness of them in the life of the church. Spiritual relations are sovereign."[8] When we view the guilty person in Christ, we realize that we all stand on equal ground since we are all sinners saved by grace.

Maintain a proper viewpoint of God.

A forgiving fellowship in Christ is also fueled by two truths. First is the love of God. The appeal to forgive in Christ in verse 9 is said to be "for love's sake." Senator Mark Hatfield once remarked, "We love others because we have been shown, in our lives, that people do not need to deserve love, nor do they need to earn it."[9] None of us can lay claim to God's love based on our own merit or initiative. It has been given freely and undeservingly to us in Christ. Therefore, not to forgive others in Christ is to claim for ourselves a prerogative God does not have. God has promised that in Christ we will always find forgiveness. Therefore, in Christ, we must always seek to be forgiving.

Second, a forgiving fellowship in Christ is fueled by the assurance of the providential care of God. Paul reminded Philemon, "For perhaps he [Onesimus] was for this reason parted from you for a while, that you should have him back forever, no longer as a slave, but more than a slave, a beloved brother, especially to me, but how much more to you, both in the flesh and in the Lord" (v. 15-16). By looking beyond the surface, Philemon found the unmistakable and unshakable hand of God, guiding and orchestrating the circumstances of life to promote Philemon's good and His glory.

The arsenal of providential care provides great support when the hurts are particularly deep. Joseph found it to be his source of strength against potential embitterment toward his brothers who had sold him into slavery. When they came face-to-face with him in Egypt, the brothers feared for their lives. Surely he would not be able to forgive them, they thought. But Joseph responded, "Do not be afraid, for am I in God's place? And as for you, you meant evil against me, but God meant it for good in order to bring about this present result, to preserve many people alive" (Gen. 50:19-20. Joseph did not deny their sin or shrug it off as if it had not hurt, but he did forgive them. He had chosen, rather than to hold on to the hurt, to sift it through the hands of providential care. It made all the difference.

It is this fortification of a loving, providential overseer that affords the greatest insight to the challenging task of forgiving in Christ. Fanny Crosby, one of the greatest hymn writers the church has ever known, tells in her autobiography of a doctor's tragic error which led to her blindness when she was only six weeks old. Yet, in the years that followed she affirmed, "But I have not for a moment . . . felt a spark of resentment against him because I have always believed . . . that the good Lord, in his infinite mercy, by this means consecrated me to the work that I am still permitted to do."[10] And indeed, her hymns written in physical blindness have continued to illumine the church as to the "blessed assurance" we have in Christ.

STEPS TOWARD FORGIVENESS

TO THE GUILTY PARTY

• Recognize that your actions toward others make a clear statement about your fellowship with God.

• Make sure you are not hiding behind your Christianity. If you need to write or call someone to rectify a wrong you have done, do it today.

• Start with saying, "I'm sorry." It sounds so easy for those who have never tried it. It is a good place to begin.

• Remember that nothing is worth forfeiting the peace of God in your life.

TO THE INJURED PARTY

• Do not shrug off or ignore the hurt. No real healing can ever take place this way. Acknowledge that you have been wronged.

• Concentrate on God's unmerited love and providential care. The tendency, once you acknowledge the hurt, is to become overwhelmed by it. But this will threaten to engulf you with a sea of self-pity. Maintaining a focus on God will give you the overriding perspective you need. Genuine healing and restoration flourishes when the pain is conquered by God's grace.

Corrie ten Boom survived imprisonment at the Ravensbrück concentration camp. She had experienced firsthand the beatings and barbaric conditions. She had seen many die, including her own sister, from cruel treatment. Yet she had also seen there the power of Christ. The message she carried from Ravensbrück was that no pit is so deep that Christ is not deeper still. As she traveled throughout Europe speaking to various churches, she made that message known. One day after she spoke at a church service in Munich she recognized a former S.S. man who had stood guard at the shower room door in the processing center at Ravensbrück.

He came up to me as the church was emptying, beaming and bowing. "How grateful I am for your message, Frau-

lein," he said. "To think that, as you say, He has washed my sins away!"

His hand was thrust out to shake mine. And I, who had preached so often to the people in Bloemendaal the need to forgive, kept my hand at my side.

Even as the angry, vengeful thoughts boiled through me, I saw the sin of them. Jesus Christ had died for this man; was I going to ask for more? Lord Jesus, I prayed, forgive me and help me to forgive him.

I tried to smile, I struggled to raise my hand. I could not. I felt nothing, not the slightest spark of warmth or charity. And so again I breathed a silent prayer. Jesus, I cannot forgive him. Give me Your forgiveness.

As I took his hand the most incredible thing happened. From my shoulder along my arm and through my hand a current seemed to pass from me to him, while into my heart sprang a love for this stranger that almost overwhelmed me.

And so I discovered that it is not on our forgiveness any more than on our goodness that the world's healing hinges, but on His. When He tells us to love our enemies, He gives, along with the command, the love itself.[11]

How can you forgive when the hurt runs deep? It's not easy, but it is not impossible. In Christ there is the call to forgive. In Christ there is the power to forgive. Remember: there is no hurt so deep that the Cross of Christ is not deeper still. His love and care will sustain you. By the grace of God in Christ, let us get on with the business of forgiving one another and press on in the fellowship of God's peace and in the fellowship of God's people.

seven

Philippians:
Maintaining Joy in Christ

On the morning of March 3, 1513 Spanish explorer Juan Ponce de León struck out in search of the "fountain of youth." On April 11, he thought he had finally found it by discovering Florida. He returned to Spain to secure the title to the land and returned again to Florida in 1521. While he was attempting to come ashore, he was mortally wounded by the Indians. Unfortunately, Ponce de León was not the first or the last to be destroyed in pursuit of the fountain of youth.

We constantly hear of others who go dashing off in the mad pursuit of the fountain of youth. I wonder, however, if it is the fountain of youth mankind is really looking for, or is this merely a metaphor for the "fountain of joy"? I believe most people would gladly surrender the babbling brook of youth for the perpetual spring of joy.

Max Lerner, in his study *America as a Civilization,* underscores this note. "If asked to reflect on what was their main aim in life, most Americans . . . would probably say, 'to be happy'. . . . America is a happiness society."[1]

Though this appears to be the American dream, more often than not it ends in a nightmare of disillusionment. The best-selling author Dennis Wholey, in his book *Are You Hap-*

py? observed that, at best, only 20 percent of Americans are happy. That seems a bit optimistic. Billy Graham wrote a book years ago entitled *The Secret of Happiness.* The first page is a good clue to why it is still selling.

> *A college senior said, "I am twenty-three. I have lived through enough experiences to be old, and I am already fed up with life." A famous Grecian dancer of yesteryear once said, "I have never been alone but what my hands trembled, my eyes filled with tears, and my heart ached for a peace and happiness I have never found."*[2]

Modern man is still searching for that illusive fountain of joy. Is it out there? The answer is yes, and the Book of Philippians tells us where it may be found.

LIVING A LIFE OF JOY IN CHRIST

THE SPHERE
Percy Bysshe Shelley's poem, "The Past," poignantly reminds us of man's futile attempt at capturing joy in himself. He asserts that "joy once past is pain."[3] Even when we look back with fondness at a special event or person in our life, we inevitably feel a twinge of pain because the joy of the moment is no longer a present reality but a fading memory "pressed between the pages of our mind." What a contrast Psalm 16:11 affords: "In Thy presence is fulness of joy; in Thy right hand there are pleasures forever."

Only within the sphere of Christ is there the undeniable offer of a full joy; not some fly-by-night joy, but joy full—overflowing and neverending. This is so because the joy is grounded in the eternal presence of Christ Himself. As long as He lives, happiness must exist, and He lives forever.

The major Greek word for "joy" in the New Testament is *Chara.* We come across it either as a verb or a noun no less than sixteen times in the four chapters of Philippians—amazing when you consider that in the other twelve epistles, Paul used it only thirty-six times. Add to this the fact that "in

Christ" is used twenty-one times and you can begin to appreciate the interrelationship between joy and our new life in Christ spoken of in Philippians.

THE COMMAND

The noteworthy aspect about Philippians is that rather than affirm a position of joy in Christ, it instead presents joy in Christ as a repetitive command (2:18; 3:1; 4:4). The fact that it is given us as a command is important. My position in Christ is a fact whether I reckon it true or not. I may not believe I am justified in Christ, but it does not alter the truth. This is not so, however, with my lifestyle in Christ. I cannot say that my lifestyle is joyful in Christ whether I realize it or not.

Jesus told his disciples that it was only as His joy was at home with them that their joy would be complete (John 15:11). Joy is the fruit, not the root, of my new life in Christ. If I yield daily to Him, I will walk in a path of full joy. If I reject His provisions, joy will flee accordingly.

This constant command to rejoice could be translated "Be joyful" or "Enter real happiness." Some people assert that the Bible speaks about joy, but does not address the issue of happiness. They make joy out to be the "good guy" and happiness the "villain." This is simply not the case. The Bible does not shy away from addressing the importance of happiness. Psalm 1 and Matthew 5 speak directly to the happiness of the child of God. In fact, the Hebrew and Greek words translated "blessed" in these passages have as their major idea that of happiness. Happiness should properly be viewed as a state of well-being which biblically is brought about by a proper relationship with God. Joy is actually the emotional fruit of this particular state of happiness.

This interrelationship between happiness and joy is particularly striking in Matthew 5. In verses 3-12, happiness is not portrayed as some flippant, on-again off-again emotion, but rather as a state of blessedness or well-being which comes from knowing God. Therefore, those in such a state of blessedness can still rejoice (be joyful) even when adversity strikes.

Furthermore, rejoicing can even be commanded because their
state of happiness is still intact (Matt. 5:12). It has not been
washed away, being predicated on their relationship with
God and not on the unstable sands of earthly circumstances.

It may come as a shock, but God wants to lead you into a
state of happiness and fullness of joy. C.S. Lewis went so far
as to suggest that the ultimate purpose of God in all His
work was to increase joy.

At first, you may raise a theological eyebrow at such brash-
ness, but closer reflection bears this out. Man is miserable
without God; and God could have left him in his self-im-
posed state of rebellion, but He did not. Instead He sent His
Son to die to alleviate the misery of sin and restore us to a
state of happiness in which we may enjoy once again the
knowledge of His presence. Remember: Jesus told His disciples that He had come to bring them full joy (John 15:11).
It is only appropriate, therefore, that Paul commands us to
submit to this special work of Christ.

In one of Charles Spurgeon's sermons on joy he said, "A
Christian has never fully realized what Christ came to make
him until he has grasped the joy of the Lord. . . . As heaven
is the place of pure holiness, so is it the place of unalloyed
happiness . . . and it is our Saviour's will that *even now* His
joy should remain in us, and that our joy should be full"
(italics mine).[4] It may properly be said that man is living as
God intended only when he is obedient to God's command
to experience in Christ a fullness of joy.

THE SAFEGUARD OF MAINTAINING JOY
IN CHRIST

Some would indict believers by saying their Christianity does
not keep them from sinning; it merely takes the joy out of it.
Well, they are partially right. For years we listened to sin
shouting its promises of joy like some street-wise politician
looking for support. The louder the voice, the easier to forget
the empty promises of the past. But now we see that the joy
of sin hasn't been taken out; rather the lie has been exposed

—there was never any lasting joy in sin. In place of the lie has come an abiding joy conceived in Christ, nurtured in Christ, and completed in Christ.

Philippians 3:1 asserts that this repeated command to be joyful in Christ "is a safeguard for you." This is precisely what it is. Tolstoy's famous novel *War and Peace* asserted that pure and complete joy were impossible.[5] But they are not. We have only to stop gambling our joy away on things that do not satisfy. In Jeremiah 2:13 God warns: "For My people have committed two evils: They have forsaken Me, the fountain of living waters, to hew for themselves cisterns, broken cisterns, that can hold no water." This describes man when he seeks happiness apart from God.

Whatever I perceive to be the sphere of happiness is what I will desire. Whatever I desire will be what I invest my life in. Therefore, my belief of where happiness will flourish will largely dictate the direction and pursuit of my life. The major problem with this, however, is that though belief may dictate pursuit, it cannot determine truth. Therefore, man apart from God follows a path for happiness that in the end is flawed, faulty, and fatal; in short, a broken cistern.

A young married couple came into my office under great emotional duress. The wife confessed, "I am miserable; my life is over. I think I have married the wrong person." She was thirsty and her cisterns were dry. She had thought joy would be found in the social status of a high school debutante, but it wasn't. She had thought joy would be found in scholastic excellence, but it wasn't there either. Now she is looking down into the cistern of marriage and finds it unfulfilling too. There she sat, trying to convince herself that maybe another cistern, another marriage, would quench her thirst. Nevertheless, I could tell she knew that even though she changed scripts, she would end up with the same plot, the same lines, and the same ending.

Disillusionment is inevitable when we seek a lifestyle of joy outside of Christ. The charge to anchor our joy in Christ effectively communicates that we cannot find it, in any lasting sense, anywhere else. Thus, the command is indeed a "safeguard for you." It spares us the disappointing trek down the barren path of circumstances, self-centeredness, and worldly credentials.

SAFEGUARD AGAINST CIRCUMSTANCES

In Philippians 1 Paul faced many trying circumstances, including the real possibility of death. He was unjustly being held in a Caesarean prison, awaiting a transfer to Rome to face Nero. While in prison, he tasted the rancidness of "Christian profiteering"; rivals were taking advantage of his absence by preaching the Gospel for personal gain. Yet Paul was confident that the work of God in his life and ministry would continue (1:6). Therefore, he affirms, "I rejoice, yes, and I will rejoice" (1:18). This repetition, including both the present and future tenses, was Paul's way of saying, "Rejoice? You bet I will!" William Morrice observed that "the future tense of joy indicates that the Apostle's mood is no passing emotion but that it is one that will outlast all the present troubles."[6]

No circumstantial potholes in life are too deep to swallow up the joy of Christ. In fact, just the opposite occurs. The triumphant attitude Paul expresses in chapter one is, as Karl Barth described it, "a defiant Nevertheless."[7]

I have had some counselees express a defiant "nevertheless," but not like Paul's. Theirs fell on the side of despair, regardless of what they read or heard. Paul's, however, fell on the side of joy, regardless of what others had to write or say.

Those around Paul could have listed all kinds of reasons why he should not be in a state of happiness and experiencing an abiding joy. Yet he continued to respond with a defiant Nevertheless I am at peace with my Saviour (1:2); Nevertheless He is performing a good work in me (1:6); Nevertheless He is using the circumstances of my life to promote His grace within me and to those around me (1:12-26).

Paul goes on to list three ways in which he could actively see the hand of God amid the difficult circumstances. First, he shared the Gospel with the whole praetorian guard. Second, he was given the ability to share with others who came along. Third many fellow believers developed a greater courage to share their faith with those around them.

There was actually a fourth benefit that Paul was too close to the situation to realize. During his imprisonment, he wrote four precious letters (Ephesians, Colossians, Philemon, and Philippians)—the prison Epistles. This is the triumphant power of a joy centered in Christ.

Paul could approach death with this "holy defiance." Nineteenth-century English poet Algernon Swinburne wrote in his book *A Lamentation*, "While he lives let a man be glad, for none hath joy of his death."[8] But this was not the case with Paul. Not even death could imprison his joy in Christ. Death was to be a great gain, an opportunity for him to go home (Phil. 1:21-23).

Does death threaten your joy? If your principle joy is in this life or the things of this life, you are destined for disappointment. It is all temporal; and if you care to take an honest look around you, you will admit this life is fading fast. Conversely, when we secure our joy to Christ, we will find His joy being unleashed within trials rather than wilting under them. We will also have His joy which turns even death into great gain.

SAFEGUARD AGAINST SEEKING JOY IN OURSELVES

I read of a humourous story which took place at the railway station in Providence, Rhode Island. An excited bridegroom gearing up for his honeymoon absentmindedly asked the clerk for a single ticket. His wife chimed in behind him, "Why, Tom, you've bought only one ticket." He answered without a moment's hesitation, "By thunder, you're right, dear! I'd forgotten myself completely." It was a good try. Unfortunately, it reflects a basic chord running through all of us: self-centeredness. Such music never generates a lifestyle of happiness.

Preoccupation with self will always purchase the fastest one-way ticket to unhappiness available. Psychologist Dr.

Karl Menninger once gave a lecture on mental health where someone asked, "What would you advise a person to do if they felt a nervous breakdown coming on?" To the audience's astonishment, he replied, "Lock up your house, go across the railway tracks, find someone in need, and do something to help that person."

Yet we are so programmed to view everything and everyone according to our own personal advantage that we do not realize how detrimental it is. Dr. Larry Crabb, one of the preeminent Christian counselors in America today, described most people entering marriage as falling into the "tick on a dog" syndrome.[9] Such a person goes into marriage ready to drain from the spouse all that he or she needs to be fulfilled and joyful in life. The only problem is that the partner enters by the same door. Therefore, you end up with no dogs, two ticks, and not enough blood to go around. A graphic but highly accurate picture. It seems so natural to pursue joy by what seems best for oneself, but the opposite result takes place. Man wrapped up in himself packs a very small package of joy.

Philippians 2 bears out the testimony that as we anchor our joy in Christ, we are set free from the tyranny of selfishness to serve others. This in turn promotes the daily life of joy in Christ within us. Paul admonished, "Do nothing from selfishness or empty conceit, but with humility of mind let each of you regard one another as more important than himself; do not merely look out for your own personal interests, but also for the interests of others" (2:3-4). Paul then chronicles this joyful, servantlike attitude of Christ as it was lived out among the Philippians by both Timothy and Epaphroditus (2:5-30).

The conduct of their lives speaks of a real willingness not only to serve but to be servants. There is a difference. I have known people who said they would be glad to serve but only in "high profile" positions. Helping set up chairs or teach some children in Sunday School did not qualify. Others, however, constantly amaze me with their true servant spirit. They work behind the scenes, not caring who gets the credit as long as God gets the glory. They do not take their ball and run when they do not get their way. They are servants in the New Testament sense of the word whose joy is not in themselves but in Christ.

Maintaining our joy in Christ is a significant safeguard. It sets us free from the enslavement to ourselves and in turn unleashes the fullness of His joy in us, directing us to a life of meaningful service to our family, friends, and anyone who may intersect our lives.

SAFEGUARD AGAINST CREDENTIALS

Norm Sonju, vice president and general manager of the NBA Dallas Mavericks, once stated: "I have seen many people who believe that true satisfaction is realized in the success they attain. That's not true satisfaction. The only true peace of mind is found in the things of an eternal perspective."

Paul would have given a hearty "Amen" to that. In Philippians 3:4-6, Paul listed his impeccable credentials. Culturally, intellectually, and religiously, he was in a class by himself. He was a Jew of Jews, a Pharisee of Pharisees, and had distinguished himself above his peers as he studied under one of the greatest teachers of the first century, Gamaliel. Yet when he came to Christ, he willingly gave up his "world-class ranking" in view of "the surpassing value of knowing Christ" (Phil. 3:8).

All of us face great demands on our time as we seek to maintain our walk with the Lord on the one hand and excel in the professions God has for us on the other. It is here we must be extremely guarded concerning the source of our joy. This point was driven home to me at the end of my first year at seminary. I let my devotional time get crushed under the crunch of exam week. At the end of the week the score was: exam days 5; quiet times 0. I realized I had been counting knowing Christ as loss for the sake of gaining a few extra points on my exams. So I prayed, "Lord, put me in a position this summer which will really stretch me and reflect my true priorities; and may I be found faithful to counting everything a loss in order to know You better."

Did He ever answer. Within one week I applied at a dock company in Dallas and was hired. All summer I worked from 4 A.M. until 5:30 or 6:30 P.M. Monday through Friday with an occasional Saturday thrown in for good measure. The work was long, hard, and hot. By the time I came home, got cleaned up, went out to eat (I wasn't married then) and returned home, it was close to 9 P.M. Yet I was able to maintain a commitment of getting up between 2:00 and 2:30 A.M. every morning for my quiet time. By the end of the summer, I had learned afresh that "the surpassing value of knowing Christ Jesus my Lord" (Phil. 3:8) isn't worth sacrificing for anything. Second, I had learned that the privilege of growing in Christ had become for me a bedrock of joy which no external accomplishments could match.

Nothing is wrong with worldly acclaim and credentials if they should come, but nothing is inherently great about them either. Our credentials will neither enhance or diminish a life of lasting joy in Christ. If they flow within the scheme of a Christian's priorities, fine; but if they can only be achieved at the sacrifice of growing in Christ, they must be abandoned. Worldly acclaim is too shallow a reservoir to house the treasure of lasting joy.

One day Jesus assembled the disciples together and sent them out to minister. He gave them a wide range of authority over demonic activity. When they returned, they were brimming with joy. "Lord, even the demons are subject to us in Your Name!" they exclaimed. But the Lord settled them down when He said, "I was watching Satan fall from heaven like lightning. Behold, I have given you authority to tread upon serpents and scorpions, and over all the power of the enemy, and nothing shall injure you. Nevertheless do not rejoice in this, that the spirits are subject to you, but rejoice that your names are recorded in heaven" (Luke 10:17-20).

The disciples were falling prey to a great danger—locating ultimate joy in something or someone other than Christ and His saving work. Christ was not forbidding a spirit of joy in their special circumstances, but the disciples were on the verge of taking legitimate joys and confusing them with ultimate joy. If we seek to maintain a spirit of joy from these things, what happens when they disappear? Our joy flounders in a sea of bewildering circumstances, selfish pleasures, or worldly pursuits.

The Bible tells us that happy is the man whose house is full of children. Very special joy and happiness come at the birth of a baby. The Bible tells us to rejoice in the wife of our youth. Few joys compare with that of a wedding. A legitimate sense of joy fills you through certain accomplishments that God may allow you to experience. But if you live long enough, you will see joyful births give way to weeping mothers and tiny coffins. Or joyful wedding memories shatter from broken promises and unfulfilled expectations. Or successful careers grind to a halt because someone decides that it is time for some new blood. At such times where has the joy gone? It has been driven away by the winds of sorrow, hurt, or the mere passing of time.

That is why this command to "be joyful in the Lord" is such a safeguard. Do not look for ultimate joy in broken cisterns or you too will become broken and in constant thirst.

William Borden bore a famous name and a wealthy heritage. He had within his reach all the joys this world could amass. But he traded them all in for the one satisfying joy of knowing Christ. In time this "Borden of Yale," as he is often called, chose to use his gifts, talents, and education as a missionary to China. Many thought him a fool. It was a waste of a life, many concluded.

Borden had only been gone a short while when tragedy struck. He contracted cerebral meningitis and died in Cairo, Egypt before ever reaching China. As the news broke, no doubt the contrasting images emerged. He had an opportunity for a life of relative ease, where others would serve him and where he could carve another notch for the "Borden" name; but he gave it up to die in pain, isolation, poverty, and youth. Surely, he had missed out on all the joys of life—or had he? This was not the testimony of those who were with him and ministering to him in those last days. They echoed the sentiments of one editorial which appeared after his death: "Here was a fearless spirit, not fettered by worldly wisdom in the disposition of his powers and possessions, who looked out and up, beyond all these, and grasped the really great thing of value for which to spend them."[10] Borden's spirit, as acknowledged by those around him, was at the end as it had always been. He lived life with no reserve, no retreat, and no regrets.

What a testimony to the real source of joy in life. As songwriter Bill Gaither put it, "Once you've found the source of music, you just can't help it, God gives the song." Anchor your joy in Christ, and you will find in Him the ultimate safeguard for true, sustaining happiness.

eight

Titus:
Maintaining Integrity in Christ

A certain company which sells traveler's checks has as its slogan, "Don't leave home without them." Perhaps the same challenge should be issued regarding our integrity.

In March 1980, *Reader's Digest* reported that a truck knocked down a power pole in Moncks Corner, S.C. A blackout enveloped the town. Within ten minutes, six people showed up at the utility company to pay their electric bills.

Whether it is committing grand theft or open adultery, neglecting a small bill, subscribing to *Sports Illustrated* for the swimsuit issue, using people for corporate advancement, cutting in line at the grocery store, lying at work, or fudging on your golf handicap, these are all matters of integrity.

THE CHURCH'S STRUGGLE FOR INTEGRITY

In light of the public and private scandals which have infiltrated every sector of our society, even *Time* magazine is asking what happened to Honest Abe and good ol' fashioned ethics.[1] More important questions for us are: What happened to good ol' fashioned, honest Christians, and what role is the church playing in setting the pace of integrity within society? The answers at this point are not very encouraging.

Integrity has to do with a soundness, unity, or integration between what is seen on the outside and what an object is on the inside. In today's fast-paced disposable world, integrity seems to be a rare commodity. We have grown accustomed to the labels "Simulated" and "Look-alike" to cover up the fact that they are not the real thing.

The church that I attended as a youth had four beautiful, heavy silver offering plates. As times changed and the church grew, the leadership decided that they needed additional plates. They selected two that looked exactly like the old ones except they were only silver-plated and were thus much lighter than the actual silver ones still in use. I used to love to sit and watch as the plates were passed around. Several times I can recall someone braced to receive one of the old silver plates being handed one of the lighter ones instead. The results were hilarious as money flew everywhere. Two plates had a good appearance but no integrity.

Unfortunately, this is not the only place the church displays her lack of integrity.

A CHURCH IN CRISIS

As I was preparing this chapter, an article appeared in the newspaper describing a new board game coming out on the market entitled "Fleecing the Flock." It is based loosely on "Monopoly," but rather than playing the part of a real-estate tycoon, you act out the lifestyle of a greedy evangelist. The game comes equipped with collection plates and has as its goal the collection of theme parks, record companies, and television stations. To accumulate such properties, players must try to bankrupt their unholy competitors, while keeping their own sexual escapades secret. With each sale the world must be asking, "Where is the church's integrity?"

Dr. Howard Hendricks said that he has personally investigated over 250 cases of pastoral affairs within a one-year span. Nowadays it is not the pastor worrying about adultery in the pew, but the person in the pew worrying about adultery in the pulpit. One friend summed it up when he commented on a Christian writer, "He would have served God better if he had never written a line and remained faithful to his wife."

If the leadership is corrupt, where does that leave those who follow? It becomes a classic example of the blind leading the blind; the end result is a church in crisis, with much of the salt having lost its flavor.

A CHURCH OF SUBSTITUTES

Chuck Colson was on target when he recently answered a question about the three most important ingredients in the Christian life. Without hesitation he said, "That is easy: integrity, integrity, and integrity!"[2] Who would argue with him?

The substitute of salesmanship.

There are those in the church who would tell us that if we can get some half-committed star athlete to be our spokesman, he is better than a wholehearted Mr. Unknown. Of course, such drawing power does not come cheap as we must pay the star handsomely for his appearance. A laborer is worth his wages, but a charlatan is worth so much more!

Why do so many congregations invite well-known personalities? Because the church wants to look like a winner to society. Floating around in the back of our minds is the notion that Christianity is in a loser's bracket, and it needs some external star status to give it credibility in the world's eyes.

In his book, *The Integrity Crisis,* Warren Wiersbe candidly points out, "The average Christian probably doesn't realize how important popularity is to ministry these days." He then described a situation which took place when he was pastor at Moody Church. He noticed people started coming out of the woodwork asking him to come here, speak there, or write this and that. Was it because all his rich talents had finally been discovered or was it because he was at the time the pastor of one of the most prestigious evangelical churches in America? Wiersbe knew that it was the Moody Church name that created the initial excitement.

One day a pastor called him up and wanted him to give a series of messages on worship. Because Wiersbe's schedule was already full, he graciously declined and offered him the name of a friend whom he felt would do a tremendous job. Wiersbe recorded the rest of the conversation this way:

> *"I've never heard of him!" the pastor said.*
> *"So what?" I replied. "Until this evening, I'd never heard of you! Are you looking for a celebrity or a speaker?"*
> *My friend never got the invitation.*[3]

When we need anyone other than Christ to boost our credibility in the eyes of the world, we do so at the sacrifice of our integrity. The only name worth "dropping" in a conversation is the name above all names: Jesus. After all, when you are friends with the King, how important are the pictures of princes on your wall?

The substitute of ability.

If these church experts cannot sell us on the book "People to Know," they will turn to its sequel, "Things to Know." In this book we are told that success is governed by our sheer talent and brilliance. I had a Christian leader once assert that if I knew the original biblical languages, I would be more effective for the Lord than someone who did not.

Though I majored in Hebrew in seminary, I disagreed with him. All things are never equal; therefore, the premium must always rest with cultivating a life of integrity.

The pressures to play Christianity by the rules of the world are great. Therefore, we must make a decision to resist placing the measuring rod of success for our life or ministry on the external. The spiritual strength of our ministries must never be gauged by slick presentations, aesthetic surroundings, and high-profile visibility. Nor can we allow ourselves to fall into the trap of testing our spirituality and usefulness strictly on how much knowledge we can accumulate, learning we can master, theology we can process, or success we can achieve. God will often overlook the marquee of stardom, the wizardry of a high IQ, and the spellbinding captivation of flashy talents, but He will not overlook integrity.

We do not need to wonder why the world sticks to the substitutes as long as the church herself is living by them. Therefore, it is time that the church awake and fall to her collective knees and ask God to show her again the role of integrity in Christ. I believe that when we do this, we will find the instruction which Paul gave Titus to be at the heart of integrity.

INTEGRITY: AN INTERNAL MATTER

A GOD OF INTERIOR DESIGN

That God is absolute integrity is conveyed in the opening verses of Titus. Paul wrote about "the hope of eternal life, which God, who cannot lie, promised long ages ago" (1:2). Scripture consistently affirms the inability of God to lie or to deceive. Therefore, when we read the Bible we do not have to say, "This is what the Lord appears to be, but I wonder what He is really like?" What we see is what He is. He will never appear to be hurt and displeased with rebellious sinners while in reality He is nonchalant and cavalier in His judgment of sin. He will never appear to be so loving as to graciously forgive any sinner who comes in the name of Christ and then not do it. He will never appear to care for us as we go through trials and struggles while actually being detached, aloof, and indifferent to our burdens. What God has revealed Himself to be outwardly in His dealings with man is nothing more than the reflection of who He is inwardly.

A LIFESTYLE THAT BEGINS WITHIN

God is concerned that His children reflect a life of "interior design" as well. The exhortation in Titus to be people of "good deeds" is repeated no less than six times (1:16; 2:7, 14; 3:1, 8, 14). Yet, the exhortation is not merely a call to whitewash old sepulchers; rather "good deeds" are designed to be an outward reflection of a new soundness within. In Christ, God shows His priority of making whole people from the inside out. Titus 2:14 states that Christ "gave Himself for us, that He might redeem us from every lawless deed and purify for Himself [literally, in Himself] a people for His own possession, zealous for good deeds."

In Christ we have finally developed a unity or integration between what we are inwardly and what we exhibit outwardly. This is why we are called on to "adorn the doctrine of God our Saviour in every respect" (Titus 2:10). The word *adorn* is *kosmeō*, from which we get "cosmetic." As it is used in the New Testament, though, it does not mean to cover up our new life in Christ like some teenager trying to hide her freckles; rather, it is an exhortation to take what you possess and cause it to stand out. In fact, Kenneth Wuest in his *Expanded Translation* accurately renders the word with the phrase "embellish with honor."

When Jesus was comparing the kingdom to the ten virgins, He spoke of the five who were ready as having trimmed (in Greek, "adorned") their lamps (Matt. 25:1-13). They were commended for being ready and for having cut the wicks in such a way as to allow the full beauty and brightness of the light to shine forth. They did the things outwardly that would allow the light within to glow more radiantly.

Recently, I read of a local church that had gotten quite tired of a farmer who would drive his tractor across their parking lot as a short-cut to get to his other field. They decided to take matters into their own hands and agreed to erect a fence to stop the nonsense. The move solved their initial problem. Unfortunately, it did little to adorn the Gospel. They did not heed Paul's advice "to malign no one, to be uncontentious, gentle, showing every consideration for all men" (Titus 3:2).

After a while, the church members felt convicted about what they had done, so they quietly took down the fence. The farmer was so moved that he came to church, and after hearing about the one who could change their hearts to love even a man like him, made a decision to accept Christ. The church had trimmed the wicks and the farmer had seen a glorious light.

This is the great business of each of us in the church—to

adorn the relationships and situations of our lives with a knowledge of Christ which will allow His presence within to shine forth. This can be done as we focus on the grace of God brought to us in Christ.

THE ROLE OF GRACE

Dr. Donald Campbell, president of Dallas Seminary, wrote a letter to the alumni in 1987 in which he talked about the crisis brought on by all recent scandals within the church. He issued the challenge that "by the grace of God, we can avoid the clutches of impurity." We tend to read such a statement and think *Cliché,* but is it?

The grace of God is the backbone of integrity. To reduce it to a cliché is to insure paralysis within the church. The New Testament finds it impossible to give practical advice for living apart from the inward working of the grace of God in Christ.

Titus 2:11-14 tells us that the grace of God has come, bringing inward renewal, outward reform, and a secure hope, in that order and all in one package. It is not the "graces" of God in Christ, as if we can pick and choose the aspects of "in Christness" we want. The same grace that has saved you in Christ, equips you in Christ, and will ultimately perfect you in Christ.

Some think that the real power of the church for the present is in conjuring up some unholy alliance with the power brokers of the world. But this will never get the job done. Do not underestimate the power and priority of God's grace in the present for witnessing to the world around you. "The Church is not influential because she is able to manipulate the affairs of the State. The Church is powerful in the measure in which she is revealing the truth of God in her own life."[4]

For this reason, God cares so much about ethical conduct. It is a part of the overall statement to the world as to what His grace in Christ is all about. Ethical conduct is the handwriting on the wall, the open declaration of what He can do inwardly to a heart and life.

Trying to stand on the grace of God in Christ for your past
and future but not your present is a precarious balancing act.
It is like climbing onto a three-legged stool to share Christ
while somebody underneath you is sawing off one of the
legs. Eventually you will crash, and the world will walk away
having been amused but not directed to the Gospel.

Rest assured, the grace of God is one package tied together
in Christ. The same grace which has the power to possess
you and secure you will also produce in you an adornment
befitting of His gospel.

INTEGRITY: PRACTICAL IMPLICATIONS

ADHERENCE TO GOD'S BOUNDARIES
The Boundaries.
The hub of Titus is found in 2:11-14 as the epistle locks in
on what our identification in Christ will promote within us:
salvation, expectancy, and good works. The rest of the book
spirals from this center. Boundaries of attitude and behavior
are established for the believer regarding leadership positions
within the church (1:6-9); handling rebellion within the
church (1:10-16; 3:8-11); relating to different age-groups,
the opposite sex, differing social strata, the government and
the unsaved around him (2:1-10; 3:1-7).

Adherence to these boundaries would radically change
some of the approaches many have toward ministry. There
are Christian organizations that sanction a continued separation of Indian believers by caste even within the walls of the
church. These groups argue that it is extremely difficult to
witness to a person in the Brahman caste if you lead him to
believe that within the church there is no distinction between
him and the lowest pariah. Similar arguments have been put
forth for church-supported apartheid in South Africa. Yet,
when the arguments are weighed in light of Scripture, they
are shown for what they really are: long on rationale and
expedience, and short on integrity.

We cannot afford to sweep integrity out of the church to
bring others in.

The Need.

G.K. Chesterton philosophically warned us not to take down a fence until we know why it was up in the first place.[5] In Christ, God has established these boundaries of integrity because the lust and power of life can corrupt us as quickly in Christian service as it can anywhere else.

Every now and then I will hear a young believer tell me, "I wish I could stay home and study my Bible during the day like you. Then I could overcome some of these struggles I face on the job from 9 to 5." I guess they think I live in some isolation tank free from temptation and struggle.

The grass may look greener on the other side, but we all face the lust of the flesh, the lust of the eyes, and the boastful pride of life. To enter full-time Christian service as a comfortable buffer to temptation is to assure failure. If you are trying to run away from something, the ministry is no safe refuge in which to hide. Flee instead to the protective care of God and submit to His boundaries. There you will find relief. You will not find it hiding behind some pulpit, or in the bylaws of some Christian organization, or in the jacket cover of some Christian book.

Every believer, minister and layman alike, has the same responsibility and need to "put on the Lord Jesus Christ, and make no provision for the flesh in regard to its lusts" (Rom. 13:14). If I think I can store up an ample supply of Christlikeness and then coast to the finish line with my flesh a passive observer, I will be sadly mistaken. I must live each day under the power and authority of Christ and never leave a door cracked or a light burning for the flesh. If I do, the flesh is sure to find its way back home in my life, regardless of how spiritually mature I have become.

Practically speaking, making no provision for the flesh boils down to daily submission to God. It involves a willful dying to the wide open spaces which are pursued by my flesh, and a willful choosing to live within the boundaries established by God.

If you are constantly evaluating your actions by criteria other than the boundaries of God's grace, you will eventually lose your integrity in Christ. The reason is simple. Regardless of how carefully you avoid sin, there will come a day when the circumstances are right for it; when all the bases appear covered and no one on earth will suspect a thing. Under such circumstances, I do not believe there is any criteria except the willful submission to the boundaries of God's grace which will sustain you. Therefore, before you come to that bridge, you must settle the issue that your life in Christ has established for you the boundaries of integrity. They are for your good and they must not be disassembled. A life of integrity begins when our overriding concern is the fact that God sees. It becomes an adornment when the knowledge that God sees us is all the knowledge we need.

AN EYE ON GOD'S TIMING

Paul reminded Titus to "let our people also learn to engage in good deeds to meet pressing needs, that they may not be unfruitful" (Titus 3:14). As has already been established, deeds are not classified as good simply by their actions. What constitutes good deeds is whether they flow from a life of integrity. It is this integrity in turn which promises a fruitful life and ministry.

When Jesus approached the lone fig tree beside the road, He was hungry. From a distance He could see its leaves. Since fig trees will produce the leaf and the fig at the same time, He had every right to expect some fruit. Instead He found a tree full of leaves and barren of figs. Therefore, Jesus cursed it for its deceptiveness (Matt. 21:18-19). Today, we are seeing a lot of flower in the evangelical church but very little fruit. How sad that most evangelicals are slow to realize the difference.

Fruit rarely flourishes overnight; flowers often do. It is not uncommon for God to take many years to fashion in His servants lives of usefulness. Yet we often approach such a process with impatience. Our response is "OK, God, I will try it your way: faithfulness, integrity, the whole nine yards; but if it does not get me to the top quickly enough, then I will have to do it my way."

We may not use such blatant terms, but the end result is the same. We can get so busy building our little empires in the name of Christ that the kingdom of God becomes a stepping-stone for the kingdom of Me. Slowly our lifestyle and integrity deteriorate to that of the Pharisee whom Jesus spotted in the temple. Everyone could see him praying, but Jesus knew he was merely praying to *himself*—no fruit, just flower (Luke 18:11). Jesus may see us "in the temple" working up a nice sweat but only conclude, "Merely serving *himself*—no fruit, just flower."

God has never been nor ever will be a slave to our timetable. He cares much more about shaping our character than He does about shaping our careers. After all, careers come and go, fizzle and fade, but the development of character remains an adornment of the Gospel throughout all generations.

A life of integrity awaits God's season for fruitfulness. Joseph had to season in a field, in a pit, in Potiphar's house, and in prison, but it was merely preparation for bearing fruit over a nation. So it is with a man of integrity.

Before I finally made a full surrender to Christ's control in my life, I went through a period of rebellion. God then sent a man of integrity my way. He would come over to talk about the Bible, and I would seek to drag him into a debate which I knew I could normally win.

How then could he have been used of God to get me back on course? That's easy—he never lost his integrity. Meanwhile, I would walk away from this man of God thinking, *If I won the debate, why do I feel like I am the real loser?*

His willingness to have his life girded with Christlike integrity brought me to my knees. I discovered from him that if you do not know an answer, you may only lose a debate; but if you lose your integrity, you have lost everything.

Integrity in Christ—don't leave home without it.

nine

1 & 2 Timothy:
The Spirit to Persevere in Christ

One of the most rewarding things about ministry is to see those with whom you have shared or aided in spiritual development continue in their faith. Conversely, one of the most difficult things is to see those who have not only staggered, but thrown in the towel.

Why is it that some people exercise great commitment in the face of tremendous trials while others quit over the smallest obstacle? As a freshman in college, there were ten men who had real input in my spiritual growth. By the time I had graduated and headed off to seminary, five of them were no longer walking with the Lord. One had been my very first Bible study leader. Not everyone who starts well finishes well.

I believe all of us have the desire to finish well, though in truth, not all will. Therefore, our study in Christ brings us to this all-important issue of perseverance.

THE CHALLENGE OF PERSEVERANCE IN CHRIST

THE NEED FOR HONEST EVALUATION
Timothy held a very special place in Paul's heart. Timothy, his mother, and grandmother, had been converted under

Paul's ministry at Lystra. On Paul's second missionary journey, he took Timothy under his wing and found in him a faithful companion and minister of the Gospel (Acts 16:1ff). But that was at the early beginnings of Paul's work, around A.D. 49–50. By the close of A.D. 66, Paul penned his last letter under the inspiration of God before his execution at the hands of Nero. He was then writing to a mature son in the faith who had had sixteen years of hard ministry under his belt.

Paul's mind traversed the years of co-laboring for Christ. He reminded Timothy of how special those early days of his faith were (2 Tim. 1:3-5). Yet Paul is no daydreamer. He is acutely aware of those who have defected from the work, exemplified by the lives of Phygelus and Hermogenes (2 Tim. 1:15). Therefore, he turned to Timothy and, bracketed by fond remembrance and painful defection, exhorted him to "kindle afresh the gift of God which is in you" (2 Tim. 1:6).

What does this exhortation tell us about Timothy at this time? The expression "kindle afresh" can be translated "to keep in full flame." The image is not that of an ember which has gone out, but one that does need to be fanned back to full strength. As Donald Guthrie remarked, "There is no necessary suggestion, therefore, that Timothy had lost his early fire, although undoubtedly, like every Christian, he needed an incentive to keep the fire burning at full flame."[1]

In the midst of defections all around us, we need an exhortation to consider our own lives and ministries, for the fire can diminish with subtle ease. When Hannibal of Carthage routed the Roman legions, winter was approaching. The war was suspended therefore, and his soldiers wintered in Capua, the city of luxury. As a result they got confident, complacent, and careless. When the war resumed, they had lost their ability to fight effectively and so were defeated. Certainly we can all fall prey to a type of status-quo Christianity where we do not think overtly about quitting, just coasting. We don't necessarily yearn for the valley of sin, but we simply stop reaching for the heights of maturity.

I was on cloud nine for several weeks after having made my commitment to dedicate my life to full-time Christian service. Then a college senior hit me with some hard reality by way of a velvet glove. He casually mentioned, "Barry, I have only been involved in the ministry for a year, and unfortunately, I will be leaving soon. You have so much greater potential as a freshman to learn, grow, and be discipled, if only you continue on."

My first reaction was to say, "Who do you think you are and what do you mean by 'if?'" By the end of the year I understood what he was saying about continuing on. He gave me a challenge I have never forgotten. It has forced me to constantly and soberly monitor where I am in my walk with God from that time on. The stark reality between good starts and bad finishes all around us demands that we carefully monitor where we are at spiritually every day of our lives.

A good check of your spiritual development is to examine your "excuses." There is a tendency to make excuses when we are not where God wants us to be and doing what He wants us to do. The area of obedience could be as simple as going to church or as big as fleeing adultery. Often times, instead of obeying the Lord, we try everything imaginable to justify our lifestyle. We must recognize that using excuses is a tell-tale sign that our perseverance is floundering.

AN AWARENESS OF OUR SOURCE FOR PERSEVERANCE

Monitoring our spiritual perseverance is one thing; having the strength to do something about it is another. I have always been puzzled by Christians who quote from Winston Churchill's famous three-word speech ("Never give up!") as they exhort one another to perseverance. They treat determination as if it were the crucial factor. Not withstanding its importance, determination is not the number one factor. Just ask Peter, who denied Christ to a servant girl after stating his determination to die, if necessary, with Christ (Luke 22:33-34).

Challenge met without power or resources often works in the opposite direction. Rather than promoting perseverance, this type of challenge becomes a breeding ground for defection. If England had not been convinced that its people had adequate power and resources to defeat Hitler's Germany, such a challenge to "never give up" would have been met with laughter, not resolve. In the same vein, if Christians are not convinced that they too possess the necessary power and resources, the challenge to persevere becomes a classic exercise in futility. Here an awareness of our life in Christ is pivotal.

Since 1 and 2 Timothy share many of the same ideas, as Paul pours out his heart to his son in the faith, we will combine the two epistles and focus on the challenges given in 2 Timothy. The term "in Christ" is used seven times in this short book. The book concerns itself with the enabling grace Christ gives to live out the Christian life—grace to start well, continue well, and finish well. This can be seen in 2 Timothy 2:1 where the major challenge of the book appears: "You therefore, my son, be strong in the grace that is in Christ Jesus."

What type of strength is Paul speaking of? The Greek noun for "might" is *dynamis*. We recognize that we get the English word "dynamite" from it. The verbal form often translated "be strong" (as is the case in 2 Tim. 2:1) is actually an intensification of this word *dynamis*. In the New Testament this verb speaks of the capacity of someone to perform a demanding task either physically or spiritually, as well as describing the energizing force behind that capacity. This energizing force is none other than the work of Christ in our lives (cf. also Eph. 6:10; Phil. 4:13; 1 Tim. 1:12; and 2 Tim. 4:17).

From a New Testament standpoint, any exhortation to "be strong" is not an appeal to gut-out perseverance in the energy of the flesh but rather to rely solely on the strength which comes from our exalted Saviour. The race, as Hebrews 12:1-2 reminds us, can only be run as we focus on Christ, the author and ongoing perfecter of our faith. As we lock in on Him and His power at work in us, we enter a position of perseverance. For the Christian, ultimate strength is not to be found in numbers but in Christ through whom we can do all things (Phil. 4:13) and apart from whom we can do nothing (John 15:5).

WHAT PERSEVERANCE IN CHRIST INVOLVES

RESPONSIBLE TO GOD

Our perseverance in Christ involves two major truths, the first of which is our responsibility to God. Timothy is given one final charge by Paul to "fulfill his ministry" (2 Tim. 4:1-5). It is a charge both given and received in the presence of God. No one perseveres in his walk with God without a clear picture of his responsibility to God. Many are surprised to hear that. True, salvation is strictly a work of God on behalf of sinful man. Yet salvation also establishes a relationship, and all relationships carry responsibilities.

In a recent Bible study I asked people to come up with verses which grant Christ the title "Saviour." To their own surprise, they had a hard time coming up with many. Then I asked them to come up with verses that call Christ by the title "Lord." They found that a much easier assignment for a simple reason. The title "Saviour" is used for Christ only 24 times in the New Testament. The title "Lord" is used 433 times, including 16 times in 2 Timothy.

A view of His lordship is essential; though we stand in a Father/child relationship regarding His care and saving grace in our lives, we stand in a Master/servant relationship regarding our responsibility to Him. God has every right, as our Master, to require us to fulfill our ministry since He has empowered us in Christ to do so (2 Tim. 4:5).

It is critical that we come to grips with our responsibility to God. When Moses was in the wilderness, God commissioned him to be His spokesman to Pharaoh. But Moses was hesitant; after all, Pharaoh was no small fish. Moses said, "Please, Lord, I have never been eloquent, neither recently nor in time past, nor since Thou hast spoken to Thy servant; for I am slow of speech and slow of tongue. . . . Please, Lord, now send the message by whomever Thou wilt" (Ex. 4:10, 13).

What a string of excuses! He reminds the Lord of his oratory deficiencies and adds that, at that very moment, he was still stumbling over his words. The clincher comes when he seeks to bow out gracefully by telling the Lord, "I'm thankful and honored that You would consider me, but I think it best if You find someone else."

Then the Bible says that "the anger of the LORD burned against Moses" (Ex. 4:14) Why? The answer is found in the name by which Moses had addressed God. The chart below designates the three principle names of God in the Hebrew Bible with their English counterparts and their points of emphasis.

Hebrew Term	English Translation	Point of Emphasis
Yahweh	LORD (small capitals)	Personal relationship
Elohim	God	Power and might
Adonai	Lord (capital *L* only)	Master/ servant

Moses was calling God *Adonai,* "Master" (Ex. 4:10, 13). Yet he had the nerve to tell Him to go find someone else to do His bidding. A servant does not have such prerogative; he has the responsibility to obey.

Our faithful Saviour is our Lord, and we bear the responsibility to please Him first, foremost, and forever. To lose sight of this is to falter in the battle of perseverance. When Luther fearlessly withstood the Emperor with the famous words, "Here I stand, I can do no other," he was bearing witness to this truth. Once Hugh Latimer was preaching in Westminster Abbey and King Henry VIII happened to be in the congregation. In the pulpit he soliloquized, "Latimer! Latimer! Latimer! Be careful what you say. The King of England is here!" Then he continued, "Latimer! Latimer! Latimer! Be careful what you say. The King of Kings is here!"[2] Truly, the essence of perseverance in Christ begins with a clear sense of our responsibility to Him—first, foremost, and forever.

Within this relationship with the Master, I am thankful that even if I should fail in my responsibility, God will not fail in fulfilling His responsibility to us. "If we are faithless, He remains faithful; for He cannot deny Himself" (2 Tim. 2:13). As His children we can be assured that He will care for us, comfort us, and save us forever (cf. Heb. 2:9-16). Yet, such comfort in the faithfulness of God should not negate, but rather enhance and facilitate, my responsibility to Him.

REWARDED BY GOD

Second Timothy 4:1, 6-8 affirms that just as we are responsible to God, so too shall we be rewarded by Him. Apart from the extended benediction in 2 Timothy 4:9-22, these are the last words of spiritual instruction ever recorded for us by Paul. You can learn a lot about life by listening to someone who only has a few words left to say, for they reveal the truth about the man and his values. When death is imminent, people do not waste ink or breath on the trivial.

A few years ago the tail section of a Japanese 747, flight 123, was damaged during flight and the pilots lost control of the airplane. It zigzagged across Japan for forty-five minutes until it eventually crashed into the side of a mountain, killing all but a young girl and a stewardess in the back of the plane. At the crash site, several handwritten notes were discovered on the back of sickness bags and airline magazines. Bereaved families of six of the victims received a measure of comfort when notes penned by their loved ones just before the crash were discovered. One husband wrote, "Machi Ko, take care of the kids." Another victim, Kenchi Matsumoto, could manage but three words to his two-year-old son: "Jetsuya, become respectable."[3] Not surprisingly, none of the notes concerned such trivial matters as weather and sports. Instead, the words went straight to the burden of the heart.

Paul is doing the same here. He does not ask Timothy, "What are your latest programs and budget figures?" Rather, his burden is for Timothy's faithful ministry and where he was headed spiritually. Paul was writing to an individual who may have only been going through the motions at the time, and so his last words to him were, "Timothy, don't stay down; nothing can compare with the finish of this course. I know—I'm there!"

In my years of ministry I have heard many express regret that they did not live more faithfully for the Lord, or come to know the Saviour sooner. But I have never heard one individual say to me, "I think I have given too much to the Lord during my lifetime. I regret the investment of time and energy I have made in service to the Lord." Somehow, I do not believe that I shall ever hear it.

Perseverance in Christ is the best investment we can ever make with our Christian life. We can never outgive a gracious and rewarding God. He will reward even a cup of water given to a little child in His name (Matt. 10:42). First Corinthians 15:58 holds out the promise, "Therefore, my beloved brethren, be steadfast, immovable, always abounding in the work of the Lord, knowing that your toil is not in vain in the Lord."

The Greek word for "vain," *kenos,* describes a man who has been caught empty-handed. He made great promises, but when push came to shove, he was found empty-handed. Such will never be the case with our great God. No matter how great the toil, the reward will always exceed a hundredfold. David Livingstone had a firm grip on this principle. His sacrifices and perseverance in service for Christ are legendary.

Yet, as he told the students of Cambridge University in 1857: "Can that be called a sacrifice which is simply paid back as a small part of a great debt owing to our God, which we can never repay? . . . Away with the word in such a view, and with such a thought! It is emphatically no sacrifice. Say rather it is a privilege. . . . I never made a sacrifice."[4]

DEEPENING OUR PERSEVERANCE IN CHRIST

MAINTAIN AN OPEN IDENTIFICATION WITH THE GOSPEL

In 2 Timothy 1:8-18 instead of urging Timothy not to be ashamed of the Gospel, though he has said it elsewhere

(Rom. 1:16), Paul now exhorts Timothy not to be ashamed of the *testimony* of the Gospel. Here the focus is on the testimony, which is different. The Gospel is all about God's choice to save sinners by grace through the death of Christ (Eph. 2:8-9). Our testimony, on the other hand, is the ongoing effect that the Gospel has on us.

In one sense our testimony is both old and new. It is old in that it is always based on the saving grace of God we experienced the moment we turned to Christ as our Saviour. It is new in that it is ever expanding and changing as daily we encounter people, situations, and circumstances that must be met with and shaped by what Jesus Christ has done for us on the Cross. Your testimony (the impact of the Gospel on your life) must not be confined to going to church or, for that matter, to any specialized compartment of your life. You cannot put your testimony under lock and key without sentencing your perseverance to death. Perseverance demands an unleashed testimony.

MAINTAIN A SINGLE-MINDED OBJECTIVE
Once while Dr. Samuel Johnson was being shown through a great castle and around its beautiful grounds, he pointedly remarked, "These are the things which make it difficult to die."[5] The great paralysis of perseverance is entanglement "in the affairs of everyday life" (2 Tim. 2:4).

Oftentimes, we do not realize the real threat of everyday or ordinary entanglement until the situation becomes quite perilous. Years ago, I read a newspaper article about a lady who wore so much jewelry that she nearly strangled to death when she tried to remove all of it. Now, that's entanglement. But spiritual entanglement is by far the most devastating because it saps us of the strength God has given to finish the race well.

Testimony and single-mindedness go hand in hand. We must have the mentality of a good soldier whose one purpose is to "please the one who enlisted him as a soldier" (2 Tim. 2:4). A few years ago there was an airlift of soldiers from Fort Bragg, N.C. to Honduras. A newspaper article described how two soldiers missed the births of their children because of the week-long exercise. In fact, one of the women was already in labor at the hospital when the call came for her husband to leave. He stayed by her side as long as he could, but eventually had to leave, only hours before she gave birth. Such commitment to duty represents true disentanglement.

I am not suggesting that husbands abandon their wives in the delivery room, but I am saying that if we have divided loyalties as to our central focus in life—to please God—perseverance will be an impossibility. Perseverance in Christ is out of the question if we do not deal decisively with anything that would rival our Saviour.

MAINTAIN A WORKMAN'S AVAILABILITY

The flip side of disentanglement from the lure of everyday living is simply maintaining a life of availability. Paul warns, "Be diligent to present yourself approved to God as a workman who does not need to be ashamed, handling accurately the word of truth" (2 Tim. 2:15). The verb *approved* carries the idea of "usefulness."

In 1535, Miles Coverdale wrote the dedication to the first English-language Bible to be published. It was a monumental achievement to his years of labor, toil, and vision. Yet many found fault with him since he was not the scholar of Greek and Hebrew they would have liked to see do the job. "One critic of Coverdale called him 'a very ordinary and plodding sort of man,' of whom 10,000 could be found any day in London."[6] So why didn't God use one of those other 10,000 people in the city? Or better yet, why didn't God use one who had greater training and more talent? I think Coverdale knew the answer. He was an available workman; the others, unavailable cynics. It is availability that God finds irresistable. It is this spirit of availability that promotes perseverance.

As available workmen, we should give our attention to "handling accurately the word of truth" (2 Tim. 2:15). To handle the Word accurately is to allow it to accomplish its purpose in your life. Brilliant exegesis is not so much an

exercise in intellectual craftsmanship as it is a spiritual discipline of carefully crafted application for your life. Such exegesis constitutes perseverance.

There is one other aspect of this issue of usefulness that
should concern us here. Paul did not treat those he ministered to as notches on his belt, but rather as his joy and
crown, his children in the Lord (cf. 1 Thes. 2:20). Furthermore, though Paul was one of the "giants," we never get the
impression that those who served under him ever had the
feeling of being used for Paul's own portfolio. Paul habitually
underscored the usefulness of those around him (cf. 2 Cor.
8–9). He saw them as part of the team—as fellow workers,
fellow servants, fellow soldiers, and fellow laborers for the
Lord (cf. Phil. 2–4).

The tenderness with which Paul exhorts others to fulfill
their own ministries surely heightened before them his view
of their own unique usefulness before the Lord. Timothy was
not fulfilling Paul's ministry or vision. He was to fulfill his
own before the Lord. I believe that, particularly with multi-
staff ministries, if we could avoid the tendency to slip into a
"production priority" mentality and instead exhibit the attitude of care toward one another's person and ministry that
Paul showed, we would have fewer casualties in the ministry.
If those to whom we minister sense that we value *their* work
for Christ, we will have played a significant role in helping
them press on in Christ. We must never forget that usefulness and being used are on opposite ends of the spectrum.
One promotes perseverance; the other stifles it.

MAINTAIN AN AWARENESS OF THE COST
OF FOLLOWING CHRIST

When Jesus spoke of the four soils in Matthew 13, He told
how a sower threw seed on rocky places. That soil represented "the man who hears the word, and immediately receives it
with joy; yet he has no firm root in himself, but is only
temporary, and when affliction or persecution arises because
of the word, immediately he falls away" (Matt. 13:20-21).
The threat of persecution has always been used to hamper

perseverance. Therefore, Paul is up front in communicating: "And indeed, all who desire to live godly in Christ Jesus will be persecuted" (2 Tim. 3:12).

Zvi is a Jewish believer living in Jerusalem. He escaped the Warsaw ghettos established by Nazi Germany as a young boy and fled to Israel at the end of WW II. His interest in Jesus as the Messiah escalated during his early days in the Holy Land. One day he went to the pastor of a Jewish fellowship of believers meeting in Jerusalem and asked him to explain the way of salvation. Moshe Kaplan expressed real delight in telling him that all he needed to do was open his life up to Christ, but first warned: "If you accept Jesus as your Messiah and Saviour, you will be in for trouble." Zvi answered carefully, "I am very sure that this is what I want to do. As far as the suffering goes, I have read about how much He suffered for me. It will be a privilege to be allowed to suffer for Him."

Over the years Zvi has endured much, but he has never been shaken. After all, once a believer has settled the issue of what is worth dying for, he has in effect determined what is worth living for. Revelation 12:11 reminds us that one of the ways we overcome Satan's attempts to thwart our spiritual progress is by not loving our lives even to death.

As we seek to maintain an open identification with the Gospel, a single-minded objective of living for Christ, a workman's availability, and an awareness of the cost of following Christ, we will find as Timothy did, a deepening strength and renewed vision for the long haul.

As I look back, I have been disappointed to see some believers fall by the wayside. However, I have also been greatly encouraged to see some who have faltered get back up and finish the race well. It is never too late.

John Mark had gone with Paul on the first missionary journey. Yet for reasons unknown to us he deserted the team (Acts 13:13). It was a terrible blot on this young man's life. Yet, almost eighteen years later Paul told Timothy to bring Mark to him because he was useful for the ministry (2 Tim. 4:11). What a turnaround. What a wonderful testimony of perseverance.

This same spirit is exemplified in the life of Thomas Cranmer. He had become the Archbishop of Canterbury in 1533. Having mingled with the reformers of Germany and having read Luther's books, he became a leading spokesman for the Reformation in England. After Queen Mary secured the throne, Cranmer was destined for a series of imprisonments, persecutions, and inevitable death. Because of his fear of death at the stake, he yielded to the pressure to renounce his former reformed positions as "all manners of heresies and errors." Afterwards, he was ordered to trial. It proved, however, to be a sham, serving only as a forum for his enemies to gain leverage against the Reformation movement by having Cranmer publicly acknowledge his written recantations. But to their surprise, rather than recanting, he renounced what he had recently done as being under duress and fear of death. He boldly stated, "And I renounce as false and untrue all such papers signed with my hand since my degradation, wherein I have written many things untrue. And forasmuch as my hand hath offended, writing contrary to my heart, therefore this my hand shall first be punished; for when I come to the fire, it shall first be burned." He was dragged off to the stake. When the fire began, he held out his hand unflinchingly toward the fire. His eyes were lifted toward heaven and he was heard repeating, "This was the hand that wrote it—this unworthy right hand."[8]

Though you may have faltered and stumbled badly, it does not mean you have been knocked out of the race. God is the gracious God who finds availability irresistible. Like a John Mark or a Thomas Cranmer, you can get back up and finish well. It is never too late to submit yourself to a lifestyle of perseverance in Christ. Exercise the strength you have in Christ; fulfill your ministry. This is your responsibility to God, and He will reward you for it. Not everyone who starts well, finishes well. Decide today, therefore, that by the power of God's enabling grace in Christ you will persevere in Christ.

ten

2 Corinthians:
The Thrill of Victory in Christ

Vienko Bogatej is probably one of the most widely recognized men in the world of sports today, and yet few people know him by name. He is the ski jumper who is pictured every week on the opening of ABC's "Wide World of Sports." His head-over-heels tumble off the imposing ski jump has left an indelible impression of "the agony of defeat."

Of course, the more recent and very tragic story is that of Donnie Moore. He was an all-star pitcher for the California Angels, who committed suicide after being haunted by his home-run pitch in the 1985 playoffs. His world became a constant downward spiral of perceived defeat. But such agony and despondency is not confined to athletes. Even those in the church feel it.

A despondent spirit is not uncommon for those serving the Lord, be it in a Sunday School classroom with spitballs and paper airplanes filling the air or home Bible studies with people who are never at home. If I were to be honest, I would have to admit that when things have not gone as I would have liked them, or I thought I should be seeing more fruit for my labors, I have thought about quitting. I sat in my college dorm room and thought about giving up the ministry. I sat in a seminary classroom and thought about giving up the ministry. I have sat in my church office and thought about giving up the ministry.

At such times I have been forced to turn to 2 Corinthians, which clearly establishes the connection between our life in Christ and the importance of our ministry. This epistle describes a real ministry in Christ and what we can anticipate the ultimate end of such a ministry to be. I believe that as we come to grips with these two aspects of ministry, we will be able to experience the thrill of victory which God has for us in Christ.

CHARACTERISTICS OF A MINISTRY IN CHRIST

Perseverance and victory are very much interrelated; however, there is a difference as related to perspective. Perseverance has to do with our march; victory has to do with the destination. Perseverance looks at what needs to be done during the battle; victory looks at what I hope the outcome of the war to be. Victory, then, can only be determined when everything is said and done. As we shall explore in the second half of this chapter, victory is assured for any ministry in Christ. We may illustrate it this way. If prior to World War I and II, insider information were passed on to me which would allow me to say categorically that victory is assured for America, you would want to know such things as who and what constituted "America" so that you could make sure you were on the victorious side.

Now then, Paul is going to assure us that victory is the final outcome of any ministry in Christ. Therefore, it would behoove us to find out exactly what a ministry in Christ looks like. Second Corinthians 3–5 points us in that direction. Ministry in Christ involves both the message and the messenger.

THE MESSAGE: TRANSFORMING
A ministry in Christ is fundamentally centered in a message: the death, burial, and resurrection of Christ. Second Corin

thians 3 brings out the fact that the glory received through the Law fades, but the glory that comes through Christ is unveiled and increasing. We bear the victorious message that by faith in Christ a person becomes a new creature and is placed under the peaceful reconciliation of God (2 Cor. 5:17-21).

Therefore, a ministry in Christ begins with the right message. If we should shy away from the distinctive message of the uniqueness of Jesus Christ, there can be no ministry in Christ regardless of how sincere our humanitarian efforts or sacrifice might be.

Dr. Harry Ironside, the great expositor of the twentieth century, told the story of Dr. Charles Berry, who was on the cutting edge of liberal thinking during the early years of his ministry. He felt at liberty to substitute the message of salvation by faith in Christ with a message of salvation by morality and ethical conduct. But suddenly people in his congregation noticed a change in his preaching. Years later he related what caused the change.

One stormy night a lady came to Dr. Berry's door asking if he were a minister. She begged him to come help her mother. He could tell she was from the slums, so he tried to convince her that one of the missionaries in her area would do quite nicely. But she would have none of it. Since he could not dissuade her, he finally relented and went out in the rain with her.

When Berry met the young lady's mother, he realized that she was dying. The mother looked up at him and asked, "Can you get me into heaven? I've been a great sinner, and I don't know how to get in."

He started to pontificate on the virtues of living a good life, to which the lady responded, "You don't understand, Sir! That won't do! I'm dying and I've lived a bad life. It's too late for me. Oh, can't you get me in?"

Berry tried again by reciting various moral platitudes. Again she exclaimed, "That won't do! I'm a poor sinner! I've no time to lead a Christian life. Oh, can't you tell me how I may get into heaven?"

He had nothing else to offer her. He had come to the end of his system and it was shown to be bankrupt for a needy soul. In desperation he decided to share with her some of the Gospel stories that his mother used to tell him in his childhood. So he began to tell her of a wonderful Saviour who had died to redeem lost sinners.

The woman listened and finally exclaimed, "That's it! That ought to get me in, shouldn't it! Did He die for sinners? Then that should get me in." She then knelt down and trusted Christ as her Saviour.

Years afterward Dr. Berry explained, "I helped get her in that night, and while I was helping to get her in, I got myself in also!"[1]

It is time to turn back to the one message that alone bears the stamp of God's victory over death and hell—the blood of Christ. As we stick to this message we will place our ministry squarely in the center of the only lasting train of triumph.

THE MESSENGER
Our spirit: humble.
The subject of chapters 4 and 5 of 2 Corinthians moves from the message to the messenger. The spirit of the messenger comes into the forefront as 2 Corinthians 4:1-7 speaks of God having chosen to place the great treasure of the Gospel in "earthen vessels, that the surpassing greatness of the power may be of God and not from ourselves."

You can visit certain places in the southeast corner of Jerusalem where you will find broken pottery fragments dating to the time of Christ and before, simply lying neglected in the dirt. Nobody bothers to pick them up because the pottery is so common and so fragmented as to be worthless. It is precisely this type of pottery which is indicated by "earthen vessels." There was never any glory in an earthen vessel. Any significance it had came from what was stored inside.

As God's children, we are earthern vessels. The glory doesn't originate within us. We are no different, better, or more valuable than any other people on the face of the earth. The difference rests in the treasure we hold. A person who will refuse to partake in a ministry because it appears beneath him has confused the treasure with the vessel. Such an attitude is uncharacteristic of a minister in Christ and stands in juxtaposition to the label Paul and others gave themselves— "bond-servants for Jesus' sake" (2 Cor. 4:5). The label of "bond-servant" would probably not be one of the credentials necessary for a listing in "Who's Who," but God reveals it will solidify a listing in the "Who's Ministering in Christ" category.

The depth of your spirit constitutes a significant ministry in Christ. If you engage in humble service, you will have a ministry in Christ because you will be reflecting the very heartbeat of the ministry of Christ (Phil. 2:1-11).

Our outlook: eternal.
One thing that can keep us from being crushed when we are afflicted, or despairing when we are perplexed is an eternal perspective (2 Cor. 4:1-18).

Oliver Goldsmith dedicated one of his poems, "The Traveller," to his equally talented brother, Henry, who had given himself to serve the Lord. In the dedication, Oliver wrote: "I now perceive, my dear brother, the wisdom of your humble choice. You have entered upon a sacred office, where the harvest is great, and the labourers are but few; while you have left the field of ambition, where the labourers are many, and the harvest not worth carrying away."[2]

It grieves me to see people leave a ministry not because of some shift in the direction of God's will, but due to the passing winds of circumstances or comfort. Jesus warned that "night is coming, when no man can work" (John 9:4). When Jesus collects the harvest of our years to measure for eternal substance, what will He find? We may amass what we consider a great harvest in the fields of ambition, status, and recognition. But in the end when Christ comes and we see that harvest for what it is worth, not even we will want to carry it with us. We will cry out, "O Lord, let it lie; it is only ashes" (see 1 Cor. 3:10-15).

A ministry in Christ leaves the ashes of temporal activity

behind and invests instead in the genuine gold of work for
Christ. It seeks to carve the mark of Christ into our homes,
neighborhoods, workplaces, and churches. It does so by
maintaining the value of an eternal reward as a touchstone
for ordering the daily affairs of life.

Our goal: pleasing God.
The overriding ambition of a ministry in Christ is that
"whether at home or absent, to be pleasing to Him" (2 Cor.
5:9). This must be our ultimate goal because "we must all
appear before the Judgment Seat of Christ" (5:10).

Often a ministry can degenerate into an exercise of jug-
gling everyone's "happiness" rather than enjoying God's. We
receive people's praise too easily and their criticism too reluc-
tantly, while paying only passing attention as to how all this
is playing out in the throne room of heaven.

One affluent church was having a summer intern fill in for
its minister. The intern did well in his sermons but often
would let his prayers slip into a grammar-poor cry from the
heart. Finally, the board decided to confront him and told
him that they found it very difficult to listen to his prayers
because of his grammar. He responded, "It's OK; I wasn't
praying to you anyway!" He knew with whom his ultimate
accountability lay. Placing the focus to where it belongs—on
pleasing God—provides us with contentment about our ministry, regardless of the varying responses from the outside
world.

Paul had told the Corinthians earlier, "Therefore do not go
on passing judgment before the time, but wait until the Lord
comes who will both bring to light the things hidden in the
darkness and disclose the motives of men's hearts; and then
each man's praise will come to him from God" (1 Cor. 4:5).
How exciting amid the grind of day-to-day ministry to realize that when our pleasure is in pleasing God, our praise,
though perhaps long left dormant by the world will come
from Him.

The right message delivered in the right spirit with the
right outlook and goal determines whether a ministry is in

Christ or not. In light of the promise that awaits us, we must be very clear on what constitutes a ministry in Christ.

THE PROMISE: A MINISTRY IN CHRIST IS TRIUMPHANT

THE GREAT CONQUEROR

Dr. Harold Willmington, vice president of Liberty University, shared the story of an Indiana farmer who was a die-hard Republican. Back during the elections of 1936 he told his wife that he was going to ride the several miles into town to listen to the election returns. He warned her, though, to get busy packing up all their belongings because they might have to move out of the county. She was startled, so he explained: It looked as if the county was going to go for Roosevelt, and the farmer was bound and determined not to live in any county that would choose a Democrat. In town he huddled around the radio to listen to the election returns. Early in the evening he sent word back to his wife to stop packing. She asked the messenger, "Does this mean the Republicans have won?" The young man replied, "Oh no, Madam, it means there ain't no place to go. Roosevelt's done taken it all!"

Christ too has taken it all. Second Corinthians 2:14 depicts Christ as the great conqueror as it exclaims, "Thanks be to God, who always leads us in His triumph in Christ."

Such an image in Paul's day was a powerful one as it drew on the famous Roman "Triumph." This "Triumph" was the highest honor a victorious general could ever receive. After having conquered a foreign foe, in whose territory peace was established and a positive extension of the empire was gained, the general would return home to a glorious celebration. He would ride through the streets in a chariot drawn by four horses and be draped like royalty. He would hold the ivory scepter in his hand, and on his head would be a crown. The crowds which lined the streets would cheer, and his soldiers would march behind him in full army dress wearing their decorations for battle and shout, "Io triumphe!"

This glorious scene is the ongoing victory of Christ.

Though some today wish to do away with such imagery, He is the one true victor of heaven and earth. One denomination wanted to omit from their hymnal, "Onward, Christian Soldiers" because they said "Jesus was the Prince of Peace and not the supreme field commander."[3] The Bible does not support such an assessment. Christ went to the cross as the unblemished lamb of God (1 Peter 1:19), but when all the returns were in, the grave was empty and death had been defeated. Yes, He went to the cross as a lamb, but He conquered death like the lion from the tribe of Judah (Rev. 5:5). Christ has taken it all.

REALM OF AUTHORITY ESTABLISHED

Christ stood in triumph on the Galilean mount and proclaimed that all "authority" had been given to Him (Matt. 28:18-20). As H.B. Swete, a renowned Bible scholar of his day, noted:

> *The field of Jesus' authority seems to grow as His ministry advances; at the outset He has authority to forgive sins on earth; as the days pass on, we read of authority to act as the final judge of all human lives, to determine the bounds of His own life, laying it down and taking it up at pleasure; on the eve of the passion He speaks of authority given to Him over all flesh, i.e., all mankind. But none of these great claims reaches the boundless magnificence of the words 'All authority is given to me in heaven and on earth.*[4]

Knox summed it up best, "He was given heaven and earth to do what He liked with them."[5]

What has He chosen to do with regard to His authority on earth? He has summoned us to be a part of a victorious mission, a mission of spreading His triumph everywhere. When He stood on the mount and commanded His disciples to go into all the world and make disciples of every nation, He wasn't using hyperbolic speech. The commission was a grand, all-encompassing one because His victory was an all-encompassing one. He has taken it all. Christ triumphant without human weaponry, resources, or finances charges us with spiritual world conquest by the twofold spiritual means which rest squarely on His shoulders: His power and His presence. He is the supreme field commander.

IMPLICATIONS OF A MINISTRY IN CHRIST

NOT LOSING HEART

The hardships, struggles, and fatigue from the battle have sometimes loomed larger than life, and we begin to wonder if our service really matters. At such times we must fortify our hearts with God's promise: our labor is not in vain.

Paul affirmed, "For as many as may be the promises of God, in Him [Christ] they are yes; wherefore also by Him is our Amen to the glory of God through us" (2 Cor. 1:20). When we think of the special promises of God to us, we tend to think of the blessings of eternal life and the like, and well we should. However, one area of God's promises often overlooked involves our ministry to Him. In 2 Corinthians 2:14 we have the promise that God "always leads us in His triumph in Christ, and manifests through us the sweet aroma of the knowledge of Him in every place." Our ministry has going for it the assurance of ultimate victory.

If I am playing a baseball game in which I am behind by one run in the bottom of the ninth inning, my spirits would be high because I know the game can still be won. However, if the score is 15–0, I would just want the game to get over with. But what if I knew ahead of time that we were going to score 16 runs in the last inning? My confidence would not be shaken even though we had taken a terrible beating for eight and a half innings. My positive attitude would not be related to the score at the moment, but to the knowledge of the final outcome.

Paul and his companions were "afflicted in every way, but not crushed; perplexed, but not despairing; persecuted, but not forsaken; struck down, but not destroyed" (2 Cor. 4:8-9). To top it off, Paul even bracketed such hardships with the, affirmation "We do not lose heart" (2 Cor. 4:1, 16). Why? Was it because Paul and his companions were great warriors and could snatch victory from the jaws of defeat? No. It was because they rested first in the knowledge of the final outcome promised by God. "And such confidence we have through Christ toward God. Not that we are adequate in ourselves to consider anything as coming from ourselves, but our adequacy is from God, who also made us adequate as servants of a new covenant" (2 Cor. 3:4-6). God's yes in Christ provides the assurance of the final score.

No matter how long we labor, no matter how difficult the task, no matter how receptive the audience, we must not buy into the diabolical lie that Satan is marching over our ministry in Christ, shouting, "Io triumphe!" It may be his wish, but it will never be his reward. On the contrary, the promise of God assures us that He always oversees our ministry in Christ, guaranteeing its victory. The promise does not mean we will be free from setbacks or bouts of discouragment, but simply that the victory procession is present, continual, ongoing, and assured. Christ stands with all authority, and the promise of victory is an emphatic yes in Him.

Second, Paul and his companions found strength as they went through trials by drawing on the comfort from God. They knew Him to be the "God of all comfort; who comforts us in all our affliction so that we may be able to comfort those who are in any affliction with the comfort with which we ourselves are comforted by God" (2 Cor. 1:3-4). The Greek word for "comfort," *parakaleō*, either as a noun or verb is used 74 times in Paul's letters. Quite surprisingly, we run across it 29 times in this letter. Second Corinthians is an epistle of God's abiding comfort in the midst of trials and hardships. It speaks of the God of comfort who comes to our aid and whispers, "Don't despair; I promise victory is imminent."

We cannot allow ourselves to become like Saul, who gave up on Samuel's coming too soon (1 Sam. 13). Saul's defeat was not in the battle, but in giving up hope and becoming disobedient. God has promised that we will be led in triumph; let us therefore not lose heart. We need to stand at whatever post God has given us and draw comfort for the present and assurance for the future.

Jesus admonished us not to take the hand off the plow (Luke 9:62), even when we think it isn't going anywhere. There were times early in my church-planting ministry when it all seemed to dangle on the thinnest of threads, and collapse was a week away, if not sooner. But each time, God reminded me that the thickness of the thread was unimportant. Whether or not He held it was important. Furthermore, even if that particular ministry were to collapse, it was only one inning—not the whole ball game. It is always better to give yourself to a cause that will ultimately succeed than to throw away your life on causes that do not bear the stamp of eternity.

Scripture promises us that when we are operating within the will of God, we have the ultimate victory. Don't ever turn your back on a ministry because it is not progressing as you'd like it to. To lose heart is to lose perseverance; to lose perseverance is to forfeit victory in Christ.

We know that if we take our hands off the plow, we will not be "fit for the kingdom of God" (Luke 9:62). The Greek word for "fit," *euthetos,* is found in only two other places in the New Testament (Heb. 6:7 and Luke 14:35), and in both cases it is translated "useful." We are not talking about losing salvation, but of privileged usefulness in Christ's train of triumph. To maintain the hand to the plow is the one sure guarantee of sharing in the ultimate cry: "Io triumphe!"

May the words of Galatians 6:9 be a hedge around our ministry: "And let us not lose heart in doing good, for in due time we shall reap if we do not grow weary."

HIS GRACE IS SUFFICIENT

Amazingly the vision of a third heaven played second fiddle to the thorn in the flesh in promoting the work of Christ through Paul (2 Cor. 12). Sufferings and trials often bring out a depth of ministry to which no amount of eloquence and skill can compare.

In my last year of seminary I went through a bout of total exhaustion and, as a result of not taking care of myself, a degree of depression set in. It was a very difficult time for me and even now after all the intervening years, I find it very difficult to talk about. Yet God has taken this thorn and turned it into strength. Like Paul, I have learned that my God is the God "who comforts the depressed" (2 Cor. 7:6). Furthermore, I have become more sensitive and sympathetic to those around me who may be struggling. My period of depression also led me on the odyssey of exploring what it means to be in Christ, a journey out of which this book has taken flight. I saw afresh what Augustine had seen many centuries earlier—that Christ changes all my sunsets into sunrises! All ground can be reclaimed by the victory in Christ.

Lastly, I was reawakened to the limit of my own strength and ability. Christ had spelled it out quite clearly: apart from Him we "can do nothing" (John 15:5). Yet it is often a truth we have to experience before we believe. Nonetheless, dependence on Christ is an important lesson to learn, for it is only as we exhaust our own resources that we learn there is no limit to His. Christ alone can change tragedy into triumph, pain into power, and obstacles into opportunities. It is a wonderful thing to come to the end of your abilities and discover, "I can do all things through Him who strengthens me" (Phil. 4:13).

Recognize that His grace is sufficient. Satan may have his hour, but God shall have the day.

Since we serve a triumphant Christ, we must get up and march on in service for Him. In the famous Italian naval engagement between the navies of Genoa and Venice, the Genoese admiral was handed a crushing defeat. But he did not let it crush him. Instead, he regrouped, took inventory, called for repairs, and when the ships were ready, he ordered them to again set sail to the very same place they had been routed.

"What?" asked one of the officers. "Return to the place we were routed?"

"Yes," replied the admiral. "It was rendered famous by our defeat, and I will make it immortal by our victory."[6]

Never give up on the ministry God has for you. In the weakness and hardship God is forging an eternal victory in Christ. Secure for yourself the "thrill of victory" by maintaining your ministry in Christ.

PART THREE

Anticipating a New Future

Until the Lord returns, death will overtake us. But for those of us in Christ, death cannot overcome us. How wonderful to reflect upon the fact that our new heritage and our new lifestyle eventually give way to a new destiny. God's re-creative work in Christ has a definitive climax. We are destined for a heavenly home under the protective care of God and for the ultimate transformation into the image of Christ "from glory to glory" (2 Cor. 3:18).

eleven

1 Thessalonians:
An Undying Hope in Christ

I sat in my Egyptology class at Hebrew University in Jerusalem, taking copious notes and drawing stick figures of men and birds, when my professor turned to me and in front of the class said, "I am going to be attending a Christian funeral today. Christian funerals appear so different." Then with her eyes dropping and a tone of despair in her voice, she noted, "You seem to have a hope that we do not have."

Though her words were forming statements, her eyes seemed to be asking the question, "Where is hope to be found?" I must admit it took me a moment to recover from the shock. Very rarely does someone reveal the desperate moments of her life so openly.

Why is it that authentic Christianity exhibits such a qualitatively different approach to death? The questions concerning life and death are the questions about which our life in Christ provides some solid answers. This then is our focus as we now turn our attention to the First Epistle to the Thessalonians.

OUR HOPE IS IN CHRIST

The Greek Stoic philosopher Epictetus once wrote, "A ship should never depend on one anchor or a life on one hope."[1]

In essence, "Don't put all your eggs in one basket." It is a
philosophy often adhered to today. In such a system, hope is
treated as nothing more than a Wall Street commodity about
which the philosophical brokers of the world scream at us
"Diversify! Diversify!" So we put a little hope here and a
little hope there and cross our fingers that collectively they
may all pull us through the dark chasm of death.

Yet will such a spiritual smorgasbord of wishful thinking
ever provide us with a secure hope of heaven? No! We need
something more definitive than that. But where do we turn?
What distinctive does Christianity offer a groping world?

A non-Christian attended a service with me in which the
preacher spoke on the wonderment of heaven. My friend
turned to me and rather cynically remarked, "How does he
know what is beyond the grave? He hasn't been there."

I had no problem with the question. It reminds us that
before we can talk about an unwavering hope beyond the
grave, we must have someone who has been there and blazed
a trail through it. If there is no one like that, then perhaps
Epictetus was right. The best we can do is mix it all together
and wish. But if one has blazed the trail, then we would be
foolish to place our hope anywhere else. Christianity affirms
that there is One who has, and in Him our hope of heaven
securely rests.

CHRIST, THE TRAILBLAZER

First Thessalonians spells out our hope of heaven which is all
based on what the Lord Jesus Christ has accomplished in His
death and resurrection. "But we do not want you to be unin-
formed, brethren, about those who are asleep, that you may
not grieve, as do the rest who have no hope. For if we
believe that Jesus died and rose again, even so God will bring
with Him those who have fallen asleep in [literally,
'through'] Jesus" (1 Thes. 4:13-14). Through Christ's death
and resurrection God achieved His grand design of bringing
many sons to glory and putting death to death. Hence,
Christ has become the captain or pioneer of our salvation
(Heb. 2:10).

CHRIST, THE FORERUNNER

Because Christ triumphed over the grave, He has established Himself as our one and only forerunner before the throne of God. "This hope we have as an anchor of the soul, a hope both sure and steadfast and one which enters within the veil, where Jesus has entered as a forerunner for us" (Heb. 6:19-20).

An interesting practice related to the ship and anchor could often be seen around Mediterranean seaports. In the harbor a great stone, sure and steadfast, would be embedded in the ground near the water's edge. It was called in the Greek the *anchoria* or "anchor." Sometimes a ship could not, because of its sails, make its way to a secure mooring within the harbor. In such a case, a "forerunner" would go ashore in a small boat with a line, which he would firmly secure to the anchoria. The work of the forerunner in pulling in the line would allow those on the ship to be gradually drawn near to shore.

In a similar way Jesus has been our forerunner. The Bible affirms that we were dead in the water, hopelessly unable to maneuver ourselves safely into the harbor of heaven or anchor ourselves within the veil. The winds of sin were against us. But Christ has gone past the gate of the Golden City, through the temple, and into the holy of holies. He has torn apart the veil which separated God from man, and has anchored us before the throne. As our forerunner He pulls us right into the very presence of God.

Well over a hundred years ago, Edward Mote wrote the following hymn which captures beautifully this special work of Christ:

When darkness veils His lovely face, I rest on His unchanging grace; In ev'ry high and stormy gale, My anchor holds within the veil.

His oath, His covenant, His blood, Support me in the whelming flood; When all around my soul gives way, He then is all my hope and stay.

On Christ the solid Rock, I stand; All other ground is sinking sand, All other ground is sinking sand.

Christ did not simply observe death, analyze it, quantify it, or qualify it; rather He defeated it. Therefore, the believer's hope is wrapped up in the unique person of Jesus Christ. The "steadfastness of hope in Christ" (1 Thes. 1:3)[2] makes all the difference.

MEETING THE NAGGING QUESTIONS OF DEATH

John Calvin remarked, "If anyone cannot set his mind at rest by disregarding death, that man should know that he has not yet gone far enough in the faith of Christ." The reason is because with man, the questions concerning death unfold, but the answers unravel. In Christ, the questions unravel as the answers unfold.

WHY MUST THERE BE DEATH?
The groping of man.
Apart from Christ, man can recognize the inevitability of death, but not the why. Marilyn vos Savant, who is listed in the *Guinness Book of World Records* under "Highest IQ," has a question-and-answer column in *Parade* magazine. Someone wrote to her and said, "The human body is a marvelous machine, but it sometimes arrives with various handicaps and is subject to disease and accident. What changes would you make if you were to design a new 'man'?"

Her responses was, "I don't think the human body is all that good a machine; it seems extremely fragile to me. If I were able to make a change, I would start with a body that doesn't age. I think aging is the worst disease known to mankind, because everyone suffers from it, and it's a universal killer. And it doesn't even kill you mercifully all at once when you're 100 years old; instead, it usually takes 70 to 80 years of increasing debility to do it."[3]

Apart from Christ there is an awareness of the slow deterioration of the body and the sad intrusion of death, but there still remains the inability to understand death's origin or how it may be overcome.

Granted, some have attempted to whitewash death so as to

make us believe that it is merely a part of the natural cycle of life. But regardless of how many coats are added, it can never cover up the fact that death is very unnatural and a tragic waste. It reminds me of the child who, on losing his mother, looked up with tears streaming down his chubby face and exclaimed, "Oh, how I wish there were somebody who loved me who wouldn't die."

The things that come naturally for me I do not fear. It is natural for me to eat for example, and I do not fear such an exercise. It is natural for me to enjoy the company of certain people. In their presence I do not cower in fear. So why does death elicit such a pervasive fear that stalks man throughout his life? Is it not because deep down inside we know we were created to live forever? Lurking within the recesses of our physical finitude is a scarred remnant of infinity.

This squares with the biblical account that death is an invasion on, not a part of, the natural order. As New Testament scholar B.F. Westcott carefully noted, "Death as death is no part of the divine order."⁴ It is the result or wages of sin (cf. Gen. 2:17; Rom. 6:23). Since Satan is the author of sin, the resulting death must be housed under his roof.

The answer in Christ.
But God has answered the whole spectrum of death with a new creation in Christ (2 Cor. 5:17). Though we will all die physically until the Lord returns, in Christ the sting of death (which is separation from God) has been removed (1 Cor. 15:51-58). The wages of sin have been paid and the free gift of eternal life is offered (Rom. 6:23). In Christ, death is reduced to nothing more than God's usher bringing us home to Himself.

In one of Robert Louis Stevenson's writings a man was to engage in a duel in which he was absolutely certain of death. Almost miraculously, however, he ended up surviving. As he began to walk away, his heart was singing, "The bitterness of death is past." Because of Christ's death and resurrection (1 Thes. 4:14) the bitter sting of death is past! "Therefore comfort one another with these words" (1 Thes. 4:18).

WHAT HAPPENS AT DEATH?
The groping of man.

Dag Hammarskjöld warned that "no philosophy that cannot make sense of death can make sense of life either." This is precisely the dilemma of man. Television can show us on-the-spot death. It can capture Lee Harvey Oswald being shot to death, people leaping from buildings, airplanes tumbling down runways, or space shuttles being blown apart, but it cannot give us interpretive meaning or a transcendent hope.

The world's inability to give meaning to or hope in death was well illustrated the night following the Challenger disaster. "Nightline" addressed the issue of "Kids and the Shuttle Tragedy." Jeff Greenfield raised the poignant question: "What happens to these children who are confronted with sudden, violent, graphic death literally in front of their own eyes?" He then interviewed a child psychiatrist who was called in by the school board presumably to help the children cope with the tragedy. Greenfield asked him how one should handle the tough questions the children will ask. Questions we have to learn how to answer: "Dad, what happened to those people?"

To all these heavyweight questions, this was the child psychiatrist's lame response: "They died. Their bodies were destroyed, they are no more."[5]

End of sentence, end of discussion, end of hope, and for most, beginning of despair.

Bertrand Russell asks us to carve out a meaningful life under death's "unyielding mound of despair." A losing proposition if there ever was one, but one in which man has shut himself up apart from Christ. A philosophy which flounders in understanding death has little to offer in the way of a meaningful existence. Such a philosophy reminds me of some lines from an old song, "If that's all there is my friend . . . let's break out the booze and have a ball."

The answer in Christ.

In Christ, God has taken the guessing out of what lies beyond the grave. First Thessalonians 4:13-17 gives us a precise breakdown concerning what happens at death and beyond for the one who is in Christ.

A. *The soul goes immediately to be with the Lord.* I have attended some funerals where, based on the message, I walked away unsure exactly what the state of the believer was. It is important that we be very clear here because there are a few misguided Christians and many cults which promote a view of "soul sleep" for the deceased believer.

For instance, Victor Paul Wierwille who founded the cult The Way International wrote: "No passage of Scripture teaches that there is conscious existence after death." He went on to add, "The teaching that when a person dies he immediately goes to God in heaven is one of the many doctrines of Satan and his fallen angels."[6]

This simply is not the case. First Thessalonians 4:14 says that God is going to bring "with Him those who have fallen asleep in Jesus." Now if their souls have not gone immediately to be with the Lord at death, it stands to reason that when Christ returns to the earth, He could not bring them back with Him. In 2 Corinthians 5:8 Paul says he prefers "rather *to be* absent from the body and *to be* at home with the Lord" (italics mine). The present tense of the verb "to be" in this verse is very decisive. One is either in the body or with the Lord. Furthermore, in Philippians 1:23-24 Paul contemplates his choices by saying, "But I am hard-pressed from both directions, having the desire to depart and *be* with Christ, for that is very much better; yet to remain on in the flesh is more necessary for your sake" (italics mine). Again, Paul saw that he would either be in the body, or he would be with the Lord.

These passages leave no room for confusion. If death should overtake the believer before the Lord returns, his soul goes immediately to be with the Lord.

B. *Assured a bodily resurrection.* First Thessalonians 4 goes on to say that first the dead in Christ will rise bodily from the grave (v. 16), and then those believers on the earth at the time of the Lord's appearing will be raptured to meet them in the air to be with the Lord always (v. 17).

In these verses we witness the complete reunion of body and soul in Christ. Both those who have died, whose souls are already with the Lord, and those who are alive at His appearing will be given new bodies in Christ (cf. also 1 Cor. 15:42-58).

This union of soul and body is quite significant. As we saw earlier, sin has brought, among other things, disease, deterioration, and death to the body. In effect it has marred God's creation. But in Christ, all the effects of sin and death, even on the body, must be and will be forever removed. Death will not be able to lay claim to even the smallest particle of one who is in Christ.

John G. Paton understood this. As he prepared for missionary service to the South Seas in the mid-nineteenth century some tried to dissuade him. They warned him about the risk of being eaten by cannibals. His response was, "I confess to you that if I can live and die serving my Lord Jesus Christ, it makes no difference to me whether I am eaten by cannibals or by worms; for in that Great Day of Resurrection, my body will rise as fair as yours in the likeness of our risen Redeemer.'"

Your body may be scattered on the wings of the wind or buried under the debris of time, but God has marked every particle and it shall rise again by His own almighty power. In fact, your body will rise imperishable (1 Cor. 15:42). It will never die again, for at this grand resurrection, death will be completely swallowed up in victory (1 Cor. 15:51-57).

C. With the Lord forever. Lastly, "we shall always be with the Lord" (1 Thes. 4:17).

The daughter of a friend of mine came home from kindergarten one day and hit him with a series of theological questions. She said, "Daddy, will we get kicked out of heaven if we do something bad?"

He answered, "We won't do anything bad because we will be in heaven."

To this she shot back, "But Satan did and he was an angel!"

Not often does a stockbroker get stumped by a five-year-old. However, the promise we have is that our life in Christ abides forever. The Greek word for "always" literally means "at all times." How wonderful to contemplate that our life in Christ will not simply get us there, but will keep us there for all eternity. We shall be in Him and with Him forever!

HOW DO WE HANDLE THE CAPTIVATING FEAR OF DEATH?

The groping of man.

I read the story of a single parent who found she had cancer and only had about three months to live. She asked the doctor to break the news to her young son. The doctor took little Tommy into the backyard and putting his arm around the child began to explain that his mother would be going away very shortly never to come back. The little boy, not fully understanding asked, "When does she have to go away?"

The doctor looked up and saw the large tree in the backyard and remarked, "Tommy, do you see the leaves on this tree? When all the leaves are gone from that tree, your mother is going to go away and she is never going to come back."

The doctor left thinking that he had finally gotten through to Tommy. A month later he came back to check on the family. The mother asked the doctor to speak to her son again.

"Why?" asked the doctor.

"I don't ever see him anymore," she explained.

"Why not?" inquired the doctor.

"He spends all his time in the backyard," she said, "picking up leaves and taping them to the branches!"

This desperate act of a child is no different than those who spend tens of thousands of dollars to have their bodies frozen at death in hopes that one day a discovery will be made, a cure found and, presto, they will be brought back to life, healed and youthful again.

The fear of going away for good is a terrible burden on mankind. So where does that leave the vast majority of people held captive under death's tyranny? How can they be set free? It will take something more than the straws of fairy tales and wishful thinking. It will take an authoritative word from God.

The answer found in the promise of God in Christ.
During the Battle of Britain, someone said to a man on the
street in London, "Things look pretty dark, don't they?" The
man replied, "But the King says there's 'ope, sir!" Similarly,
in 1 Thessalonians 4:15 Paul says, "For this we say to you by
the word of the Lord." How do we know for sure that there
is a glorious future beyond the dark grave for those in
Christ? The King has spoken.

Nowadays, such statements as "You have my word on it"
do nothing more than elicit a broad smile of distrust. We
know better than to trust the speaker. So how should we
respond when we read "by the word of the Lord"? Can we
take Him at His word? Or is there a credibility gap with
God?

Hebrews 6:17 affirms that God's eternal promises in
Christ are unchangeable, for it is impossible for God to lie. It
would be inaccurate to think that this were nothing more
than a self-limitation which God has placed on Himself, as if
lying were something off-limits He carefully chooses to
avoid. If God were merely limiting Himself to speak the
truth and not promising His unchangeability as well we
could never have a secure hope of what our life in Christ will
be like for all eternity. For God may accept us now in Christ,
but it would not provide a guaranteed acceptance in some
distant age to come because of the chance (if only theoretical-
ly) that God should cease in His self-limitations.

No, it has been, it is, and it shall forever be an out-and-out
impossibility for God to lie. This impossibility is spoken of
only one other time in the New Testament: Titus 1:2 speaks
of the blessed "hope of eternal life, which God, who cannot
lie [same Greek phrase as in Heb. 6:17], promised long ages
ago." Here again we have the inseparable connection between God's veracity and the believer's security. Therefore,
for those in Christ, fear of death vanishes under the clear
word from the King.

To know and believe the words of the trustworthy God
does make all the difference. After Francis Schaeffer passed
away his wife wrote:

*It was 4 A.M. precisely that a soft last breath was taken
. . . and he was absent. That absence was so sharp and
precise! Absent.*

*As for his presence with the Lord . . . I had to turn to my
Bible to know that. I only know that a person is present with
the Lord because the Bible tells us so. The inerrant Bible
became more important to me than ever before.*

*My husband fought for truth and fought for the truth of
the inspiration of the Bible—the inerrancy of the Bible—all
the days that I knew him . . . through my 52 years of knowing him. But—never have I been more impressed with the
wonder of having a trustworthy message from God, an unshakable word from God—than right then!*

*I feel very sorry for the people who have to be "hoping
without any assurance" . . . because they don't know what
portion of the Bible is myth and what portion might possibly
be trusted."*

For the one who is identified in Christ, death is no risky
business. The smoking gun of Satan is only firing blanks.
Christ has become our trailblazer who conquered death, and
as our forerunner, leads us into the very presence of God. We
are assured that at death our souls go immediately to be with
the Lord and our bodies await a glorious resurrection at His
appearing. If we are alive at the Rapture, we shall be instan-
taneously changed in Christ into a body which is imperishable and incorruptible. Furthermore, we know these things
to be true because we have God's Word on it.

IMPLICATIONS OF OUR HOPE IN CHRIST

A WONDERFUL COMFORT FOR US

Twice in 1 Thessalonians 4 and 5 Paul speaks of the comforting effect of these truths (4:18; 5:11). A secure hope in
Christ can do nothing less.

The famous preacher Alexander Maclaren got his first job
in Glasgow as a teenager. He would work in the city all week
and walk the six or seven miles home on the weekend. The

first week he went to work, his father told him to come home that Friday evening because the family would have missed him and would be quite eager to know how things went. Maclaren tried to talk his father out of it because he knew it would mean that he would have to walk through a deep ravine which was a notorious hangout for muggers in the dark. But his father insisted. All week Maclaren thought ahead to that Friday evening encounter with that dreaded ravine with all the potential danger lurking within.

Finally Friday came and he obediently struck out toward home. When he reached the edge of that dark ravine tears began to well up in his eyes. He simply could not bring himself to plunge into its abyss. As he stood there, he saw a shadowy figure coming toward him from the ravine. He was frozen with fear.

Then into the light appeared the man he loved most on this earth, his father. Next he heard, "Alexander, is that you? I didn't want you to walk this dark ravine alone, so I came to walk it with you." Maclaren remarked that what had been a dreaded terror became nothing more than a leisurely and carefree stroll as he walked home side by side with his father.[9]

If the Lord should tarry, we will all have to go through the "valley of the shadow of death" (Ps. 23:4); but in Christ you need not fear. For when you approach the valley, you will find the forerunner there to carry you through. "The Lord Himself will descend" (1 Thes. 4:16). The Lord Himself "will come again" (John 14:3). The emphasis rests on the personalized care and oversight of Christ, be it at death (as Stephen discovered, Acts 7:54-60), or at His appearing in the clouds (1 Thes. 4:17).

Our hope in Christ is a wonderful comfort for the valley.

ORIENTATION TOWARD A LIFE OF ACTION
Immediately prior to her death, someone asked Corrie ten Boom why she did not take it easy in her twilight years. She said, "I refuse to spend the rest of my life in retirement when there are so many fields to harvest."[10] What a good reminder for those who may misuse their security in Christ as an op-

portunity to complacently journey through this life.

First Thessalonians 5:1-11 shows that our hope in Christ leads to engagement, not escapism. Hope also becomes an important catalyst to personal devotion, evangelism, and social action. "But since we are of the day, let us be sober, having put on the breastplate of faith and love, and as a helmet, the hope of salvation" (1 Thes. 5:8).

I have always admired the doctors who work around deadly diseases so as to be a beacon of hope to those in need. Our hope in Christ must have the same caring effect. We should be out and about in the world as a conduit of God's grace, never as an insulator of it. Our message of hope must push us into the hurting masses who are groping for an answer to the perplexing question of death. An answer we have found anchored in Christ.

RESPONDING TO THIS BLESSED HOPE

A nurse shared with me how God brought the aspect of our hope in Christ to bear in her life. She began her nurses training as a non-Christian. One of her first assignments was to care for a dying young man. As his final days approached, she found him to be in absolute terror as he screamed and seemed to physically wrestle at times with the demonic forces around him.

This caused her to begin to ask some serious questions about life and death. But it was not until she was given the responsibility of caring for a young twelve-year-old boy that the answer appeared. This dying little boy would tell the nurses about a Jesus who had blazed a trail through death for him. When he died, the contrast was startling. There was a peaceful countenance about him as he felt the presence of the forerunner coming to take him home.

Through the testimony of this little boy she saw firsthand the qualitative answer to death found in Christ. Consequently, she turned to Christ and found in Him an undying hope for the regions beyond death.

This hope is available to you if you are in need. In Christ, death has met its final foe.

twelve

2 Thessalonians:
An Unmatched Glory in Christ

In the book *Dorie: The Girl Nobody Loved,* Doris Van Stone gives us a powerful example of victory in the midst of pain and rejection. She described how as a child she was rejected by her mother and sent to live in an orphanage where she was regularly beaten. Later, she was beaten time and again by cruel foster parents and was told daily that she was ugly and unloveable.

Dorie had never heard anyone ever acknowledge loving her—not her mother, friends, not anyone. Then a group of college students visited the orphanage and told her that "God loves you." Something clicked. She finally found someone who loved her.

As she accepted that love, her life began to change. Later in her teens a family which had begun to care for her encouraged her to see if she could locate her father whom she had not seen since she was a little girl. Dorie was in California but was able to locate her father in Tulsa, Oklahoma. He accepted her into his home and for the first time she had what she had so desperately wanted, the love of a family member.

She spent two years with him, but became increasingly aware of the fact that her heart was being cooled toward

God. Therefore, she returned to California to sort out her priorities. There she made the toughest decision of her life. She was going to serve God on the mission field. She decided to return to Tulsa to tell her father.

Dorie's father happened to be sitting on the porch when her cab pulled up to his house. She jumped out and ran to greet him.

When Dorie shared with him of her plans, he arose, turned to face the back of the porch, and said, "If that's what you plan to do, then don't unpack your suitcase. Call a cab right now and go back to California. From this moment on you are not my daughter!"[1]

It was the last time she saw him alive. Years later at his death the obituary read: no children.

The hurt of that rejection was profound. But God again met her with the promise that He would never leave her or forsake her (Heb. 13:5). Furthermore, she was given the assurance: "Dorie, your end is going to be better than your beginning."

This was a wonderful promise. In the many intervening years since, God has indeed brought to her some very special and wonderful blessings: a godly husband, a family of her own, and deliverance from the temptation of bitterness. But the ultimate fulfillment for her and all believers is yet in the future and rests in our identification in Christ.

As Dorie stated: "Surely His grace is seen most clearly against a background of rejection and hopelessness. God had displayed His love to me in a hundred different ways. Yes, there was my mother, the orphanage, and my foster homes. Yet Christ had accepted me and elevated me to be an heir of God and a joint heir with Jesus Christ."[2]

One day we will fully realize that to be coheirs with Christ is to be an heir of all things. As Arthur Pierson remarked, "God has something beyond all we have conceived, waiting for us at Christ's appearing."[3] The book of 2 Thessalonians points us to this climactic ending of all that we are in Christ. But first, before we can appreciate the end, we must develop a taste for the blessings which it will provide.

THE FUTURE OF OUR LIFE IN CHRIST

Bertrand Russell related the dialogue that F.W.H. Myers had with a friend at the dinner table. Myers asked his dinner guest what he thought would happen to him when he died. The man tried to brush the question aside but, on being pressed, replied: "Oh well, I suppose I shall inherit eternal bliss, but I wish you wouldn't talk about such unpleasant subjects."[4]

It is not the first time someone has attempted to lump the terms "eternal bliss" and "unpleasant subjects" together in his concept of heaven. I heard a pediatrician tell how, in a philosophy class, his professor had portrayed a life in heaven as nothing more than being perched on some floating cloud in some platonic state of endless boredom. The professor concluded his heavenly diatribe tersely remarking, "Who wants that?" If I had been in the class I would have been the first to reply, "Not me!"

Heaven, in actuality, will be far from boring. If you are unconvinced, it is only because you have bought into hell's rendition of it. Granted, though the Bible has a lot to say about heaven (the term being used over 700 times), it does not tell us everything we would like to know; but then again it cannot. We simply do not have the capacity to appreciate all the excellencies of heaven at this time. First Corinthians 2 tells us that our eyes have not seen, our ears have not heard, nor has it even entered our hearts all that God has prepared for us. It is God's way of saying, "You haven't seen, heard, or experienced anything yet!"

C.S. Lewis, contemplating man's inability to comprehend the sheer joy of heaven, compared it to a young child, who on hearing that his parents find fulfillment and enjoyment in sexual intimacy asks, "What do they do—eat chocolate while they're doing it?"[5]

It is a question we might expect from a child, but not from a mature adult. Similarly, we need to grow into adulthood in our understanding of heaven. It will be a beautiful place, full of unparalleled splendor, and though we cannot fill in all the details, it is important that we have a clear understanding of the parameters. For in doing so, we establish the outline of what our life in Christ will be like for all eternity.

HEAVEN IS A PLACE OF SUPREME BEAUTY (REV. 21)

To avoid the ethereal image of a floating mist, we must recognize the definitive landscape of heaven. It is described as a bride adorned for her husband. Its gates will be of pearls, its walls will be bedecked with every kind of costly and precious stone, and its streets will be of pure gold, like transparent glass.

Author Joseph Bayly once remarked, "My mother used to say that she didn't find any particular attraction in golden streets. I had no answer for her until I read a comment by F.B. Meyer that in heaven all earth's values are turned upside down. 'What do we count most valuable on earth?' he asked. 'Gold. Men live for gold, kill for it. But in heaven gold is so plentiful that they pave the streets with it instead of macadam.' "[6]

In heaven, we will never again contemplate the temptation of living for gold—only for God. There we will enjoy the creative beauty of God untouched by sin's destructiveness.

HEAVEN IS A PLACE OF SUPREME FULFILLMENT (REV. 21:4)

In counseling it is always quite sad to see someone fighting back the tears while the mate offers no comfort. It is a silent testimony to the state of their unhappiness together. How wonderful, therefore, to realize that the last tears we shall ever shed will be personally wiped away by our compassionate Father as He brings us into a state of never-ending joy (Ps. 16:11; Rev. 21:4).

In the classic work, *The Existence and Attributes of God*, Stephen Charnock is definitely on target when he notes, "Happiness depends upon the presence of God, with whom believers shall be for ever present. Happiness cannot perish as long as God lives: He is the first and the last; the first of all delights, nothing before Him; the last of all pleasures, nothing beyond Him."[7] Far from a place of endless boredom, heaven will be the home of endless joy. Since lasting joy is in Christ, our identification in Him must finally unfold into a fulfilled, unending, and uninterrupted joy forever (John 15:11).

HEAVEN IS A PLACE OF UNENDING REST AND SERVICE (REV. 14:13; 22:3)

These two aspects of heaven need to be combined lest we slip again into this notion of a bland heavenly existence. Work was not a result of the Fall but rather a part of God's creative order. Adam and Eve were given specific jobs to do long before sin ever entered the scene. What the Fall did was to bring deterioration to the value and significance of work as it corrupted work's motive, made its productivity taxing, and stripped it of permanent benefit. Heaven will restore that sense of purpose, dignity, and benefit as we render service to and for our King. In doing so, we will discover the restful contentment which fulfilling service brings.

HEAVEN IS A PLACE OF UNENDING KNOWLEDGE, HOLINESS, AND WORSHIP (1 COR. 13:12; REV. 21:27; 19:1-6)

No longer marred by sin, we will be able to give to God unbroken and rightful worship with all our heart, mind, soul, and body. For worship is essentially "all that we are, reacting rightly to all that He is."[8]

HEAVEN IS A PLACE OF LASTING COMPANIONSHIP (REV. 21:7)

Loneliness is an increasing problem in our aging society. It is so dreaded that people will often go to desperate extremes to escape it. The famous Swiss psychiatrist, Paul Tournier, told of a lady who was so lonely that she would turn on her radio just to hear the announcer say in a friendly voice, "We bid you a very pleasant good night!"

On the very day that I was finishing up this section of the book, a man came by to see me. He sat down and said,

"Pastor, you don't know how hard it is for me during the week. I'm all alone. If I could just have someone to talk to, I would feel so much better."

Such are the desperate sounds of loneliness; but the Bible promises that heaven will be a life of unending companionship with all the redeemed. I believe this truth answers the often-asked question as to whether we will recognize one another in heaven. It is hard to comprehend authentic fellowship without genuine recognition.

But more important, we will have unbroken fellowship with God. "We shall always be with the Lord" (1 Thes. 4:17). In the previous chapter we looked at how this verse related to our security. Now let us press the issue a little further. Some Christians are a little apprehensive about heaven because they have this vague notion that they will be nothing more than inanimate objects around the throne of God. Such is clearly not the case. The Scriptures view our being "with" God from the standpoint of companionship, not of mere accompaniment.

When I go on a trip, my computer may accompany me, but my wife is my companion. I do not have fellowship with my computer; I do with my wife. In heaven, we will not be the excess luggage God totes around the throne, but rather we will enjoy personal, intimate fellowship with Him for all eternity.

Samuel Taylor Coleridge, in "The Rime of the Ancient Mariner," wrote:

This soul hath been
Alone on a wide wide sea:
So lonely 'twas that God himself
Scarce seemed there to be.

For all the times we have felt distant from God, heaven is His loving way of saying, "Never again!" It is a place of supreme and unending fellowship with our redeeming God.

This is our future in Christ. Soren Kierkegaard stated that "life can only be understood backwards." But I disagree.

Your life really has no bearing unless it has a future. One psychologist commenting on teenage suicide observed, "Suicide, by and large, occurs in the absence of a sense of futureness."⁹ Life needs a future. In Christ we have all the excellencies of heaven awaiting us.

THE CLIMAX OF OUR LIFE IN CHRIST

But life also needs an ending, not in the sense of finality, but in the sense of climax. Our society lends itself to despair because, as a whole, we suffer from this loss of an ending. The Bible, however, affirms that history has a definite climax. Life is not simply a mirage, a hoax, or a cruel joke played out on the stage of Planet Earth; rather, it is a movement toward a final climax involving Christ's powerful return. "When He comes to be glorified in His saints on that day, and to be marveled at among all who have believed . . . in order that the name of our Lord Jesus may be glorified in you, and *you in Him,* according to the grace of our God and the Lord Jesus Christ" (2 Thes. 1:10-12, italics mine). The apex of history will not be some nebulous age of Aquarius safety-pinned together by some alleged harmonious planetary consciousness, but by the decisive, climatic, and glorious return of the Lord Jesus Christ.

THE CLIMAX
Three hundred and eighteen times Christ and His apostles speak of His return in the Scriptures. To excise this idea of a climatic close of history deletes one of the major teaching of Christianity. As F.F. Bruce points out, "When all the times and seasons which the Father has fixed by His own authority have run their course, God's age-long purpose which He planned in Christ will attain its fruition."¹⁰ And what is that purpose? Our glorification in Christ (2 Thes. 1:12).

Salvation is not some minor incident. Rather it is part of God's great eternal plan, the end of which is the believer's glorification in Christ. In Romans 8 we learn all things are working together for good to them that love God, because they are all pointing to this climatic end. "For whom He foreknew, He also predestined to become conformed to the image of His Son, that He might be the first-born among many brethren; and whom He predestined, these He also called; and whom He called, these He also justified; and whom He justified, these He also glorified" (Rom. 8:29-30). Second Thessalonians 2:14 refers to this upcoming glorification when it says that "it was for this He called you through our gospel, that you may gain the glory of our Lord Jesus Christ." What a gain!

THE CONTRAST
Humanism today is the failed attempt to glorify man at the exclusion of the glory of God; it cannot be done. The glorification of man by man has as its end a resigning sense of finality but no climax. Thomas Gray acknowledged as much in his "Elegy Written In A County Courtyard."

Let not ambition mock their useful toil,
  Their homely joys, and destiny obscure;
Nor grandeur hear with a disdainful smile
  The short and simple annals of the poor.

The boast of heraldy, the pomp of pow'r,
  And all that beauty, all that wealth e'er gave,
Awaits alike th' inevitable hour.
  The paths of glory lead but to the grave.

However, something worse than the grave awaits those who long for innate glory. When Christ returns, He will deal "out retribution to those who do not know God and to those who do not obey the gospel of our Lord Jesus. And these will pay the penalty of eternal destruction, away from the presence of the Lord and from the glory of His power" (2 Thes. 1:8-9). The time is coming when those who seek glory in themselves will be crushed.

There will be no glory for man except in and through the glory of Christ. It is His glory which is offered to us as gain

(2 Thes. 2:14). John Owens acknowledged: "One of the greatest privileges and advancements of believers, both in this world and unto eternity, consists in their beholding the glory of Christ." But our gain involves more than beholding; it is the active participation and mirroring of His glory. The New Testament scholar Charles Ellicott observed that the phrase "in His saints" (2 Thes. 1:10) serves very distinctly to mark not the locality of His glory, nor the instrument, but rather the mirror in which and on which His glory is to be reflected and displayed.[11]

You cannot help but sense the excitement of this climax from the pen of John: "Beloved, now we are children of God, and it has not appeared as yet what we shall be. We know that, if He should appear, we shall be like Him, because we shall see Him just as He is" (1 John 3:2). As one theologian has noted, "If the believer's destiny were not so clearly asserted, it could not be believed by any in this world."[12] Who would have ever imagined that in Christ we should become the eternal recipients of God's grace, and reflectors of His Son's glory.

THE CONSEQUENCES
The consequences which emerge from being made reflectors of Christ's glory will stand out for all eternity. First, there will be the climatic release from the sin nature. "The release from the sin nature involves a constitutional change in the removal of a force from within which has been an integral part of the believer all his days."[13] The drag of sin which constantly sought expression through the flesh all through our earthly pilgrimage will be thoroughly removed. Our reflection of His glory will never lose its luster, nor will it be even momentarily dimmed by the thought of impurity. Sin will be forever removed.

To pay my way through seminary I worked on a freight dock. Merchandise would come in from various places around the world. It was our job to unload the trucks and get the merchandise ready for distribution throughout the Dallas metroplex. Because of the various checkpoints along the way, it was a virtual guarantee that the merchandise would arrive without theft along the way. However, the potential of it arriving undamaged was another story. I picked up many boxes which I knew right away were nothing more than shattered pieces of glass. Though they had arrived, they arrived badly damaged.

In Philippians 1:10 Paul uses the word *aproskopos* to describe the condition of the believer in the day of Christ's appearing. This word was used of merchandise which arrived undamaged or of one who arrived at his destination uninjured. Our glorification in Christ will allow us to arrive in the presence of God absolutely uninjured by sin.

Secondly, our glorification in Christ will assure us an "at homeness" in heaven. The only way that we, as sinners, would ever be fitted for fellowship with God is by being made "partakers of the divine nature" (2 Peter 1:4). There is nothing else God has to offer His creatures; conversely, there is nothing else which would adequately fit us for fellowship with Him. If Christ did not present us as a bride "having no spot or wrinkle or any such thing" (Eph. 5:27), we would simply be unpresentable.

Yet the preeminent effect of our reflective glory will be so that Christ will "be marveled at among all who have believed" (2 Thes. 1:10). It would be presumptuous to think that our glorious position will vie for the center of attention in Emmanuel's land. All our radiance will merely magnify the One who could make us so radiant.

The illustration I think best represents this truth comes from my own life. When I was in high school, I was in a severe car wreck that left me two large scars on the right side of my face. I subsequently had to undergo five plastic surgeries. After one of the operations and a short stay in the hospital, my surgeon released me to return to my hometown (about 150 miles away) with a few very tiny and delicate stitches still in my forehead and cheek. He gave me strict instructions to go to one of the local surgeons to have the remaining stitches removed in about a week.

When I went to one of the doctors who was familiar with

my case, he began to look at me with a sense of awe at what had been done. In his admiration of the surgeon's work he called some of the nurses over to have a look. Each one showed amazement as they studied the right side of my face. Though they stood there looking at me, they were marveling at someone else. They were captivated with the ability of one who could perform such wonderful surgery on a person so badly scarred.

This is what our reflective glory will promote for all eternity. We will look at one another reflecting the splendor and sparkle of our sinless Saviour and marvel at Him, the One who could take creatures scarred with sin and transform them into such objects of glory and beauty. We will constantly proclaim to one another, "This could only be the work of Christ, the 'Lord of Glory' " (1 Cor. 2:8).

THE MAJOR IMPLICATION OF FUTURE GLORIFICATION

NOTHING COMPARES

The Bible does not waste time discussing the glory to come from the perspective of an armchair theologian. Discussions in both 1 and 2 Thessalonians cover the deep persecutions and trials which were being endured for the sake of the Gospel. As stated earlier, to excise this idea of a climactic close of history is to omit one of the major teachings of Christianity. But it also destroys the perspective that a believer must have in order to live out his faith in a suffering world. An understanding of our future glorification in Christ is of little benefit to us in the present if it does not translate into an ongoing force of spiritual commitment in a world which, humanly speaking, is often unfair.

Second Thessalonians 1:3-12 presents the redemptive element of suffering both from the immediate and eternal standpoints. Any suffering for Christ which we are called to endure is designed to produce a greater progress of the Gospel, a greater faith within us, and a purer love among us. This in and of itself vindicates the choices of God to allow His children to undergo unjust suffering at the hands of the world (1:3-5).

But even if we refuse to recognize this, there is still a better backdrop on which to view suffering: our glorification in Christ. One day God will settle the accounts of evil in human history and vindicate His choices eternally. That day will be for us the long-awaited time of relief and glory (2 Thes. 1:7-12).

The Greek word for relief is *anesin*. It is easy to see where our word *anacin* comes from. The promise in these verses is that final relief from pain and misery will not come from the ingenuity of man and his ability to anesthetize himself from a painful world, but from the plan of God; namely, the return of His Son in glory.

If suffering did not have this greater backdrop of glory, then we should seek to avoid difficulties and pain at all cost. But the promise of an unmatched glory in Christ allows us to make decisions based on our destiny, not our circumstances. In short, it equips us for proper decision-making.

This was one of the major purposes of the momentary unveiling of Christ's glory at the Mount of Transfiguration. Christ had conveyed to His disciples in the clearest of terms that before He would come crowned in glory He would meet the Cross (Mark 8:31-33). Furthermore, He warned that each of them must take up his cross and follow Him (8:34). He then took Peter, James and John up the mountain and for a few brief moments allowed them to see the wonderment of His unveiled glory. It was more than simply showing them His deity. It was His way of preparing them for the cost of discipleship to be paid later. A glimpse of His future glory, of which He would make them sharers, would ultimately give them the perspective they would need to endure the present. It worked. Peter and John both allude to the Transfiguration as the lens through which present difficulties are to be viewed and conquered (2 Peter 1:12-19; 1 John 2:25–3:3).

Paul also spoke of this in 2 Corinthians 4 and 11. Paul, like so many others, had constantly laid his life on the line for the Gospel. He had endured much persecution. He had been beaten with the infamous "thirty-nine" lashes five times. He had been beaten with rods three times. He had been stoned and left for dead at Lystra. He had been shipwrecked three times (not including the later shipwreck of Acts 27). He lived in constant danger and hardship. He was often hungry and thirsty, and without adequate clothing or shelter from the cold.

Yet in 2 Corinthians 4:17 he summed up all these hardships as nothing more than "momentary, light affliction . . . producing for [him] an eternal weight of glory far beyond all comparison." Imagine that! In light of the glory to come, Paul compared his present afflictions to a pesky fly at the dinner table—a minor irritant in the broader scheme of life.

A few years ago, Amy Grant made popular a song that spoke of the climactic return of Christ. She sang that even amidst the struggles and temptations of life, she believed "it's worth it all" to keep going on. Though it was a good song, I had a problem with that one phrase. To me, Scripture never conceives of present endurance in such terms. The issue is not whether it is "worth it all" to follow Christ, but rather "what can compare?"

There is a vast difference between the two concepts. If we have to stop and size up every trial and temptation which comes our way to determine whether it is "worth it" or not to remain true to God, we will at some point give up and give in. One day something is bound to come along which, in our limited understanding, seems too good to pass up. But when we focus on the ultimate relief and dazzling glory that awaits us for all eternity, our perspective changes. Our spirit becomes galvanized and our commitment steadfast as we realize that absolutely nothing can compare to the eternal weight of glory which awaits us—nothing! The suffering we must endure, the temptations we must flee are merely minor irritations or passing pleasures which hold not a flicker of comparison to what is to come. Nothing compares with our future gain: "the glory of our Lord Jesus Christ" (2 Thes. 2:14). This is the climactic promise God offers us. There is nothing else beyond glorification in Christ.

George Mueller was a great servant of God. After he was saved, God began to deal with him about becoming a missionary. But two major obstacles lay in his way—a very lovely woman whom he wanted to marry and his father. Both could tolerate him being a respectable minister in a respected community. Conversely, neither would have anything to do with him if he continued on this course of missionary service.

He began to waver, undecided as to whether full obedience to God was worth it or not. Then God brought a missionary across his path by the name of Hermann Ball. George realized that though Hermann wore cheap clothes, his mannerisms showed he had come from a family of great wealth. So he asked Hermann about this.

"Hermann told his story. Yes, his family had money. His father was a wealthy merchant in East Germany. No, they didn't understand how a man can throw away a career for Christ. He had been disinherited."[14]

George started to say, "What a great thing you have done," but Hermann stopped him. Instead Hermann responded,

You don't balance two things. You don't say—here is a life to the Polish Jews, poor, maybe even disagreeable. And here is my family with its carriages and its carpets and its rich Christmas puddings. . . . You say—God wants me to do this. So that's the only way I can be happy. No, Mueller, it isn't that I've given up so much. I've gained more.[15]

Armed with this new perspective, Mueller went back and faced the rejection of the two most significant people in his life. But again God vindicated His choices. The name George Mueller has become firmly established in the annals of Christendom while those of his father and girlfriend have faded from the pages of human history.

Time has borne the gain to Mueller. The Gospel was advanced, his own faith deepened, and the faithful love of the brethren made more precious. Beyond this, however, is the fact that heaven will be the showcase of the ultimate gain, his glorification in Christ.

As Dorie van Stone, George Mueller, and many others down through the ages have found, life will not always "be fair" at the moment, but the promise of God remains: our end will be better than our beginning. There awaits for us a heavenly future in Christ climaxed with an unmatched glory. It is a climax to which nothing can compare!

I hope that you have been helped spiritually as you have journeyed through this book. More important, I hope that there is within you a far greater desire to inculcate within your daily life all that you are in Christ. Richard Longenecker reminds us that the truth of who we are in Christ "is much better experienced than explained." How true that is (though I have waited to the end to tell you). May God give you the grace never to lose sight of your present possessions, your ongoing pursuits, and your eternal prospects in Christ.

Notes

Introduction

1. Charles Caldwell Ryrie, *Balancing the Christian Life* (Chicago: Moody Press, 1969), p. 49.
2. James S. Stewart, *A Man in Christ* (London: Hodder & Stoughton Limited, 1951), p. 157.

Chapter One

1. Warren Wiersbe, *Walking with the Giants* (Grand Rapids: Baker Book House, 1976), p. 17.
2. Vance Havner, *On This Rock I Stand* (Grand Rapids: Baker Book House, 1981), p. 43.
3. J.I. Packer, *God's Words* (Downers Grove: InterVarsity Press, 1981), p. 147.
4. F.F. Bruce, *The Epistle of Paul to the Romans* (Grand Rapids: Wm. B. Eerdmans Publishing Co., 1963), p. 102.
5. Warren Wiersbe, *Key Words of the Christian Life* (Wheaton: Victor Books, 1982), p. 16.
6. Gene Ridley, "Crown Him Lord," in *Jesus, Author and Finisher,* compiled by Morris Chapman (Nashville: Broadman Press, 1987), p. 222.

Chapter Two

1. George Leonard, *The End of Sex* (Los Angeles: J.P. Tarcher, 1983), p. 67.

2. Helmut Thielicke, *The Freedom of the Christian Man,* translated by John W. Doberstain (New York: Harper & Row, 1963), p. 10.

3. Ibid., p. 10.

4. William Barclay, *The Letter to the Hebrews* (Philadelphia: Westminster Press, 1976), p. 24.

5. John Bunyan, *Pilgrim's Progress* (Grand Rapids: Zondervan Publishing House, 1967), pp. 33–34.

6. Thielicke, *The Freedom of the Christian Man,* pp. 14–15.

7. An excellent book about the life of Chet Bitterman is *Called to Die* by Steve Estes (Grand Rapids: Zondervan Corporation, 1986).

Chapter Three

1. Don Baker, *Beyond Rejection* (Portland: Multnomah Press, 1985), pp. 16–17.

2. Arthur T. Pierson, *In Christ Jesus* (Chattanooga: AMG Publishers, [n.d.]), p. 43.

3. Arthur Custance, *Man in Adam and in Christ* (Grand Rapids: Zondervan Corporation, 1975), p. 180.

4. Baker, *Beyond Rejection,* p. 61.

5. Robert Ornstein and David Sobel, "The Healing Brain," *Psychology Today* (March 1987), p. 48ff.

6. Gary Ezzo, "Adultery," *Fundamentalist Journal* (April 1987), p. 33.

7. The only passage in the New Testament which uses the singular "saint" is Philippians 4:21: "Greet every saint in Christ Jesus." It is clear that the only reason for its usage is to indicate that within the fellowship, you cannot greet all the saints en masse and then snub any saint in particular.

Chapter Four

1. Pearson McAdarn Muir, *Scottish Divines* (Edinburgh: Macniver & Wallace, 1883), p. 82.

2. Bruce Barron, *The Health and Wealth Gospel* (Downers Grove: InterVarsity Press, 1987), p. 117.

3. Donald Groothius, *Unmasking the New Age* (Downers Grove: InterVarsity Press, 1986), p. 67.

4. Vance Havner, *Playing Marbles with Diamonds* (Grand Rapids: Baker Book House, 1985), p. 19.

5. Lewis Sperry Chafer, *Systematic Theology* (Dallas: Dallas Seminary Press, 1947), vol. III, p. 322.

6. E. Stanley Jones, *In Christ* (Nashville: Abingdon Press, 1961), p. 243.

7. C.S. Lewis, *George MacDonald: An Anthology* (New York: Macmillan Publishing Co., 1974), p. 128.

8. Warren Wiersbe, *Be Rich* (Wheaton: Victor Books, 1984), p. 30.

Chapter Five

1. John Cionca, "How Big Is Your Rug?" *Decision Magazine* (September 1988), p. 6.
2. E. Stanley Jones, *In Christ* (Nashville: Abingdon Press, 1961), p. 18.
3. *Newsweek* (August 15, 1988), p. 3.
4. Otto Friedrich, "New Age Harmonies," *Time* (December 7, 1987), p. 64.
5. A.S. Peake, "The Epistle to the Colossians," *The Expositor's Greek Testament* (Grand Rapids: Wm. B. Eerdmans Publishing Co., 1979), vol. III, p. 523.
6. D. Martyn Lloyd-Jones, *God's Ultimate Purpose* (Grand Rapids: Baker Book House, 1979), p. 43.
7. C.S. Lewis, *Mere Christianity* (New York: Macmillan Publishing Co., 1952), p. 190.
8. Audrey Hingley, "'Little Ricky' Thirty Years Later," *Christian Reader* (March/April 1988), pp. 12, 14.

Chapter Six

1. Lewis B. Smedes, *Forgive & Forget* (San Francisco: Harper & Row Publishers, 1984), pp. 126–127.
2. Brian Bird, "20 Years After Helter Skelter," *Moody Monthly* (July/August 1989), p. 27.
3. Stanley Toussaint, *Behold the King* (Portland: Multnomah Press, 1980), p. 111.
4. Ralph Wilson, "Don't Pay the Price of Counterfeit Forgiveness," *Moody Monthly* (October 1985), p. 108.
5. William Barclay, *The Letters to Timothy, Titus, and Philemon* (Philadelphia: Westminster Press, 1975), p. 270.
6. W. Graham Scroggie, *Studies in Philemon* (Grand Rapids: Kregel Publications, 1982), p. 56.
7. Ibid., p. 87.
8. Ibid., p. 50.
9. Mark Hatfield, "The Creed of Man and the Will of God," *The Other Side* (November/December 1974), p. 62.
10. Fanny Crosby, *An Autobiography* (Grand Rapids: Baker Book House, 1986), p. 24.
11. Corrie ten Boom, *The Hiding Place* (Old Tappan: Fleming H. Revell Company, 1971), p. 238.

Chapter Seven

1. Max Lerner, *America as a Civilization* (New York: Simon & Schuster, 1957), p. 693.
2. Billy Graham, *The Secret of Happiness* (Garden City: Doubleday & Company, 1955), p. 1.
3. Percy Bysshe Shelley, "The Past," *The Poetical Works of Shelley* (Boston: Houghton Mifflin Company, 1975), p. 36.
4. Charles Spurgeon, "Christ's Joy and Ours," *Spurgeon's Expository Encyclopedia* (Grand Rapids: Baker Book House, 1984), Vol. X, p. 31.
5. Leo Tolstoy, *War and Peace*, translated by Louise and Aylmer Maude (New York: Simon and Schuster, 1954), p. 1196.
6. William Morrice, *Joy in the New Testament* (Greenwood: The Attic Press, 1984), p. 126.
7. Karl Barth, *The Epistle to the Philippians*, translated by James W. Leitch (Richmond: John Knox Press, 1962), p. 120.
8. John Bartlett, *Familiar Quotations* (Boston: Little, Brown & Co., 1980), p. 633.
9. Larry Crabb, *The Marriage Builder* (Grand Rapids: Zondervan Publishing House, 1982), p. 32.
10. Mrs. Howard Taylor, *Borden of Yale '09* (Philadelphia: China Inland Mission, [n.d]), p. XI.

Chapter Eight

1. Ezra Bowen, "What Ever Became of Honest Abe?" *Time* (April 4, 1988), p. 68.
2. Charles Colson, "A Biblical View of Leadership," *Decision Magazine* (March 1987), p. 17.
3. Warren Wiersbe, *The Integrity Crisis* (Nashville: Thomas Nelson Publishers, 1988), p. 70.
4. G. Campbell Morgan, *Living Messages of the Books of the Bible* (Grand Rapids: Baker Book House, 1982), p. 261.
5. John Bartlett, *Familiar Quotations* (Boston: Little, Brown & Co., 1980), p. 742.

Chapter Nine

1. Donald Guthrie, *The Pastoral Epistles* (Grand Rapids: Wm. B. Eerdmans Publishing Company, 1978), p. 126.
2. William Barclay, *The Gospel of Luke* (Philadelphia: Westminster Press, 1975), p. 186.
3. Jill Smolowe, "Never a Year So Bad," *Time* (September 2, 1985), p. 25.

4. Samuel Zwemer, "The Glory of the Impossible," *Perspectives on the World Christian Movement,* edited by Ralph Winter and Stephen Hawthorne (Pasadena: William Carey Library, 1981), p. 259.

5. Barclay, *The Gospel of Luke,* p. 134.

6. J.D. Douglas, "The Story of Miles Coverdale," *Decision Magazine* (November 1988), p. 30.

7. Elwood McQuaid, *Zvi* (West Collingswood: The Spearhead Press, 1978), p. 173.

8. John Foxe, *Foxe's Christian Martyrs of the World* (Westwood: Barbour and Company, 1985), p. 506.

Chapter Ten

1. Harry Ironside, "The Way of Peace" (Garland: American Tract Society, 1940).

2. Oliver Goldsmith, in his dedication of the poem "The Traveller." *Miscellaneous Works,* edited by Washington Irving (Philadelphia: J. Crissy & Thomas Coperthwait & Co., 1840), p. 147.

3. Erin Kelly, "Panel hopes hymnal will bring harmony," *The News and Observer* (Saturday, April 29, 1989), p. 5. Quote from the Rev. Beryl Ingram-Ward who served on the hymnal committee.

4. R.V.G. Tasker, *The Gospel According to St. Matthew* (Grand Rapids: Wm. B. Eerdmans Publishing Company, 1978), p. 274.

5. Ibid., p. 274.

6. Donald K. Campbell, *No Time for Neutrality* (Wheaton: Victor Books, 1981), p. 68.

Chapter Eleven

1. William Barclay, *The Letter to the Hebrews* (Philadelphia: Westminster Press, 1976), p. 62.

2. The term "in Christ" is used six times in 1 Thessalonians. One other passage which, though not including the actual Greek phrase, is nonetheless translated "in Christ" by the three major translations (KJV, NASB, and NIV) is found in 1:3. There we read, "Constantly bearing in mind your work of faith and labor of love and steadfastness of hope in our Lord Jesus Christ." This verse functions like the overture of a beautiful symphony. It picks up on the three key notes (faith, love and hope) which are developed in 1 Thessalonians.

First Thessalonians 1:4-10 underscores the operation of *faith* both in and through the believers at Thessalonica. First Thessalonians 2–4:12 unfolds the Christlike *love* which is maturing within them and being worked out in their daily lives. Lastly, Paul develops this theme of a "steadfast hope in our Lord Jesus Christ" (1:3) in 4:13 and maintains this theme until his concluding remarks in 5:12-28.

3. Marilyn vos Savant, "Ask Marilyn," *Parade Magazine* (May 22, 1988), p. 22.

4. B.F. Westcott, *The Epistle to the Hebrews* (London: Macmillan and Co., 1892), p. 53.

5. Taken from the written transcript of Nightline, "Kids and the Shuttle Tragedy," *ABC News* (January 29, 1986), pp. 2–3.

6. Victor Paul Wierwille, *Are the Dead Alive Now?* (Old Greenwich: Devin-Adair Co., [n.d.]), p. 97.

7. James Allen, *The Life Story of John G. Paton in the New Hebrides* (Toronto: A. Sims, [n.d.]), p. 26.

8. Louis Gifford Parkhurst, Jr., *Francis Schaeffer: The Man and His Message* (Wheaton: Tyndale House Publishers, 1985), pp. 115–116.

9. James Reimer, "Is There Any Hope?" *Jesus: Author and Finisher,* Morris Chapman, compiler (Nashville: Broadman, 1987), pp. 154–155.

10. "News Section," *Moody Monthly* (July/August, 1983), pp. 106–107.

Chapter Twelve

1. Doris Van Stone, *Dorie: The Girl Nobody Loved* (Chicago: Moody Press, 1979), p. 78.

2. Ibid., p. 157.

3. Arthur T. Pierson, *In Christ Jesus* (Chattanooga: AMG Publishers, [n.d.]), p. 111.

4. Bertrand Russell, *In Praise of Idleness and other Essays* (New York: W.W. Norton & Company, 1935), p. 249.

5. Joseph Bayly, *The View From A Hearse* (Elgin: David C. Cook Publishing Co., 1969), p. 90.

6. Ibid., pp. 89–90.

7. Steven Charnock, *The Existence and Attributes of God* (Minneapolis: Klock & Klock Christian Publishers, 1977), p. 88.

8. John MacArthur, Jr., *The Ultimate Priority* (Chicago: Moody Press, 1983), p. 147.

9. Mike King, "Teen Suicide: A Cry for Help Heard Too Late," *Fundamentalist Journal* (April 1986), p. 28.

10. F.F. Bruce, *The Epistle to the Ephesians* (London: Pickering & Inglis LTD, 1961), p. 33.

11. Charles J. Ellicott, *A Critical and Grammatical Commentary on St. Paul's Epistles to the Thessalonians* (Minneapolis: The James Family Christian Publishers, 1978), p. 112.

12. Lewis Sperry Chafer, *Systematic Theology* (Dallas: Dallas Theological Seminary, 1947), vol. III, p. 367.

13. Ibid., vol. IV, p. 123.

14. Faith Coxe Bailey, *George Mueller* (Chicago: Moody Press, 1958), p. 26.

15. Ibid., p. 26.